Salt

and the Art of Seasoning

Previous Books

Also by James Strawbridge

The Complete Vegetable Cookbook:
A seasonal, zero-waste guide to cooking vegetables

The Artisan Kitchen:
The science, practice and possibilities

Practical Self-sufficiency:
The complete guide to sustainable living today
with Dick Strawbridge

Smoked Food: A manual for home smoking

Made at Home: Cheese & Dairy with Dick Strawbridge
Made at Home: Breads with Dick Strawbridge
Made at Home: Preserves with Dick Strawbridge
Made at Home: Curing & Smoking with Dick Strawbridge
Made at Home: Eggs & Poultry with Dick Strawbridge
Made at Home: Vegetables with Dick Strawbridge

'A cure and a tonic – *Salt and the Art of Seasoning* is a wonderfully gritty book, full of recipes I'd happily bring to the table.'

Gill Meller, author of *Outside*

'Concise and crisp, *Salt and the Art of Seasoning*'s well-written pages are likely to be useful, be it for a reason, a season or a lifetime. You'll return to it like a horse to a salt lick!'

Valentine Warner, cook, broadcaster and author of *The Consolation of Food*

'*Salt and the Art of Seasoning* is a worthy and inspirational homage to the most essential ingredient in our pantry. James teaches us how salt is the ultimate way to harness flavour, transform textures, ferment, preserve and improve our cooking.'

Eco-Chef Tom Hunt, author of *Eating for Pleasure, People & Planet*

'James has taken on writing a book about the most singularly important ingredient in the kitchen. Salt gives life. Our bodies cannot perform without salt, but that's not what I mean. I am always asked by friends and customers why my food tastes so much better than theirs. I give two answers. The first: "I have been a chef for 30 years so I'm not surprised!" The second is merely one word, "salt". Salt gives life to ingredients like no other spice. When you cook with enough salt it brings out the natural flavour so that there is no need to season it afterwards. Cooking without salt would be cooking without soul!'

Mark Sargeant, chef patron of The Brasserie MS and author of *My Kind of Cooking*

'This is an inspiring, informative and imaginative study of the most essential of seasonings in which James writes with passion and enthusiasm about this sometimes unfairly vilified ingredient in all its glory. He demonstrates salt's versatility, importance and beauty in a book brimming with recipes and projects that I can't wait to try.'
George Egg, comedian and cook

'There's so much more to salt than... salt. James Strawbridge delves into the myriad types, tastes, uses and history of salt – a seasoning that has the power to transform the flavour of even the humblest ingredient.'
Karen Barnes, Editorial Director, *delicious.* magazine

'I'm loving *Salt and the Art of Seasoning* and James's in-depth knowledge of this amazing ingredient. As a chef, salt is a massive part of my cooking, so this is a book that sits firmly on my shelf. Get yourself a salt block and try the scallop ceviche. Salt is extraordinary and so is this book.'
Andrew Tuck, chef at St Kew Inn

'I'm obsessed with salts; I collect them, write about them, cook with them, and even grow them. Just when I thought I knew all that I could about salt, Chef Strawbridge drops some delicious knowledge with *Salt and the Art of Seasoning*. Anyone who pickles, ferments, makes charcuterie, or enjoys other culinary techniques that are salt focused needs this book in their workspace.'
Jeremy Umansky, author of *Koji Alchemy*

Salt

and the Art of Seasoning

From curing to charring and baking to
brining, techniques and recipes to help
you achieve extraordinary flavours

James
Strawbridge

Chelsea Green Publishing
White River Junction, Vermont
London, UK

Commissioning Editor: Muna Reyal
Project Manager: Laura Jones
Copy Editor: Anne Sheasby
Proofreader: Vicky Orchard
Indexer: Hilary Bird
Photography: James Strawbridge, except for pages 48, 188, 281 and 288
  by John Hersey
Colour correction: Abe Olson
Food styling: James Strawbridge
Design and page layout: Luke Bird

Printed in the United Kingdom.
10 9 8 7 6 5 4 3 2 1   23 24 25 26

Our Commitment to Green Publishing
Chelsea Green sees publishing as a tool for cultural change and ecological stewardship. We strive to align our book manufacturing practices with our editorial mission and to reduce the impact of our business enterprise in the environment. We print our books and catalogues on chlorine-free recycled paper, using vegetable-based inks whenever possible.
Salt and the Art of Seasoning was printed and bound in Great Britain by Bell & Bain Ltd, Glasgow.

ISBN 978-1-915294-03-6

Chelsea Green Publishing
London, UK
White River Junction, Vermont USA

www.chelseagreen.co.uk

Contents

Introduction

A sparkle of white flakes on a seared steak in the sun. Silky smooth, buttery potato mashed with smoked sea salt. Salt falling gracefully from your fingertips onto grilled asparagus in chaotic perfection. Every pinch makes a difference to an ingredient and changes the way we eat.

I want salt to be seen as extraordinary. To be perceived as so much more than a cheap commodity and instead be seen as an essential gourmet ingredient that is as important as a chef's knife, as vital to cooking as using a hot pan. I want salt to be something you are excited about, not a last resort that is sprinkled over bland food to try and improve it as it's served.

In the past, salt enjoyed a highly prized status at our tables and was used in many ways: as a currency, as a ritual gift, to preserve food over winter and as a key ingredient within the ceremony of cooking. Yet today, salt is vilified as a risk to public health and is driven out of our diet. Many modern salts are stripped of their beneficial minerals, coated in anti-caking agents and then sold back to us either as a heavily processed sodium chloride crystal or as over-priced food supplements. In reality, in their natural, unrefined form, sea salts have the perfect balance of minerals for us to thrive, corresponding proportionally to the minerals found in our bodies and so matching our own bodies' requirements. Salt is essential for life.

Salt can lift the flavour in our food without just pumping up the sodium levels. A good sea salt, laminated with essential minerals, can enhance all the qualities of our cookery – of both its structure and taste. There are numerous examples from around the world that provide a culinary map showing us how to use salt in more creative ways, from the salted sardines of Cornwall to Eastern European sour pickles and fermented cabbage, Native American cured fish and the salt cod of Newfoundland. *Salt and the Art of Seasoning* crosses

culinary borders because salt can be applied to all areas of cooking. There are universal principles that define how we taste that have no allegiance to a particular world cuisine, diet fad or local traditions.

The word 'seasoned' means to have added an amount of salt, spices or herbs to food and it also describes when someone is accustomed to particular conditions and is therefore experienced. I feel that adding the correct amount of salt at the precise time and in the right way is what makes a seasoned chef.

Fundamentally, I want to inspire you to learn more about and reconnect with salt as a vital artisan ingredient to use at home. If I do my job, then, after reading this book, you will have learned how to use salt as a craft to enhance the flavour and texture of your food as well as to preserve, pickle, ferment and play with your food and bring out all sorts of hidden depths. With practise, you will become a seasoned cook.

The Power of Salt

We are hardwired to crave salt and told by our bodies to take it when available, so salt is a phenomenally important ingredient to understand.

Salt can also make or break a dish. No other ingredient possesses its power to alter flavour or enhance taste in quite the same way and therefore, for me, understanding how to use it is key to culinary success. By embracing the right type of salt at the right time in the right amount, you can transform food from okay to fantastic and, in my opinion, it is the major difference between a good cook and an excellent cook.

How we use salt is therefore important to our health and the flavour of all the food we cook. There are subtle ways to master salt as an ingredient that come from years of practise and research, but what I can promise is that if you take your time and read this book, work on how salt feels in your hands, really feel the sense of salt flakes rubbed between your fingers and embrace a tactile revelation that starts with touch, then your food will rise to the next level within weeks.

Over the years, I've found that there are many ways to cook a tasty plate of food. The seasoning is how the plate of food tells a story on your tongue. These messages are translated into electrical pathways, written with electrolytes that dissolve in our saliva. To look at salt as a single entity is to miss the depth of diversity that different salts from around the globe offer. A pinch of *fleur de sel* will feel and technically possess a different density and crystalline structure to, say, a grain of milled Himalayan Pink rock salt. I want to encourage you to take complete control. Own the process and with some expert knowledge and direction you can season food in a completely new way.

However, despite all care and experience, it's still too easy to ruin a dish by adding too much or too little salt. I confess that I've often over-seasoned or under-seasoned dishes. These mistakes have been formative in grasping the power of a large pinch of salt versus a little sprinkle, so the notion that we can ever take half a teaspoon or a pinch of salt and all get the same results is not how this book works.

Like a musician trying to play a harmonious chord, a chef can compose excellent food with a flick of their wrist to season in sync with a dish. When you do make mistakes with too much salt, there is little you can really do to rescue the recipe. I will suggest a few remedies, but first and foremost my advice is to add salt little by little, at intervals while cooking and to taste your food before throwing in more salt. The best approach is to take a small spoonful of what you are cooking. Taste it; if it tastes bland and feels like it needs something more to make it sing, add a tiny pinch of salt to another spoonful. Taste again. This will let you know if you need any more salt and how much to add. Punctuate food with flavour by seasoning with care.

――――

My Salt Craft

This book is essentially a collection of all my salt spells. The personal nuggets I've amassed over the years to share with you. In the right hands, salt can be alchemy for food. It is the most transformative ingredient in terms of flavour and the artisan skills I will focus on are a form of witchcraft in the kitchen.

My salt craft is shaped completely from personal experience. I'm not a salt historian or a qualified

(Above) My local Cornish Sea Salt flakes.

nutritionist. I am a chef who has explored salt in depth for several years. What I've learned about salt over the years started off in kitchens, learning the ropes first-hand as a line chef and often being told the importance of seasoning without necessarily being taught why. As I worked my way up to executive chef level, I finally found an audience for my passion for using good-quality sea salt instead of table salt. I started to fuel my salt obsession by developing flavoured salts for every occasion to sit on the pass and finish a recipe with punch. I also now work closely with salt producers, food manufacturers and chefs to teach them how to use salt effectively across all categories of cookery.

The Five Foundations of My Salt Manifesto

Firstly, all salts should taste different. If they do not, they have been so heavily processed and refined into table salt. This means they are comprised almost solely of sodium chloride and that your body will no longer recognise them as beneficial.

Secondly, unrefined or natural salt is not the enemy. There is a huge difference between a local artisan sea salt and chemically processed table salt or PDV (Pure Dried Vacuum) salt.

Thirdly, when you think of how to use salt, don't add too much salt all in one go, as it is virtually impossible to remove. Salt should be approached like an old-fashioned set of scales set on a fulcrum with imaginary weights on one arm and your ever-increasing pile of salt on the other. As you slowly add salt in layers at key stages of cooking, the balance swings a little closer to the point of perfection. You are always aiming for alignment. Season tentatively, with caution and care to begin with, until you learn where that invisible sweet spot is. With confidence, the act of seasoning can become more and more extravagant and you may find yourself playfully impersonating a TV chef at home and seasoning with the flamboyant style of a veteran chef – salt can be fun, ostentatious and theatrical. The 'Salt Bae' trend from a few years back was started by a Turkish

(Above) Large Blackthorn salt flakes from Scotland.

butcher, food entertainer and chef, Nusret Gökçe, who became a viral sensation and popular meme for his way of sprinkling salt down off his elbow onto food. He now runs a restaurant turning over millions of pounds a year, but there is room for us all to develop our own unique seasoning style.

Fourthly, exact measurements have a time and place in recipes but there is nothing more valuable than understanding your personal pinch and tailoring salt to your touch. Essentially, this is a book that celebrates empirical cooking by taste, observation, experience and touch rather than relying on antiquated measurements that tend to homogenise everything into simplistic quantities....

Lastly, I believe that we should all lean towards our local small-scale salt producers – I am proud of my blatant food-mile prejudice inspired by a personal sustainable agenda. It is a good thing to support your local artisans but, as I still love variety in this book, I will be cooking with salts from around the world without apology.

This book will hopefully provide a set of accessible techniques, methods, tips and tricks to bring out the best in all your food. All the salts in this book are personal to me. Some are extremely popular and important around the world, others drift in obscurity and are intriguing for their character. After tasting all the salts in my always-growing collection, I've become aware of how their intensity not only provides its own buzz but also awakens the inherent potential of all my other ingredients.

Don't underestimate the power of this book and I hope that you choose to practise these tricks, sleights of hand and recipe incantations at home before sharing them with your friends, families or dinner guests. Have fun and remember that part of a good magic trick is looking the part and performing with some swagger. Cook with style, a pinch of flair and make sure that you are having fun.

The Tomato Test

I see salt as a tool to bring out the very best in your ingredients. Salt has its own taste but the way it elevates and amplifies flavour is its greatest strength. Salt can reduce bitterness and sour profiles while elevating sweetness in an addictive loop of sweet, salty, sweet, salty beats.

Think of the whole cooking process like music production. You are the composer, producer, singer and songwriter. Mix in salt while keeping the levels in line. Use salt to amplify, compress, squeeze, reverb and echo. Be bold, brave and noisy, but remember that it's not an effect to apply at the end of a recording. Seasoning is woven into the ingredients like a rhythm that binds it together. Start with scales. Like a beginner. Build combinations and seasoning with a small group of ingredients before you attempt to conduct an orchestra. This is why before we go any further, I want you, please, to take the tomato test.

Salt is to a tomato what music is to dancing. I've conducted this simple taste test with Michelin-starred chefs, supermarket development teams, journalists, influencers and authors. It's very straightforward and later we will revisit it in more detail to understand the science of taste. For now, trust me and go get yourself some natural sea salt, some bog-standard table salt and a ripe tomato.

1. Cut the tomato into slices.

2. Sprinkle one slice of tomato with table salt.

3. Sprinkle another slice of tomato with the same amount of sea salt.

4. Taste the tomato sprinkled with table salt. Describe the taste to yourself. Does it taste salty? Bittersweet or harsh? What is the aftertaste like?

5. Now taste the tomato sprinkled with sea salt. How does it taste by comparison?

Mind blown? Continue reading to learn more...

(Above) Delicate sea salt flakes can easily be broken into small shards of salt between your fingers.

Salt Explained

Part One

Chapter One
What is Salt?

I live in south-east Cornwall, near the coast. When I gaze out at the cold torn waves and rocky cliffs that fall into the sea, I see the alchemy of food waiting for me. Sensory joy, strong seasonal cycles and a peaceful soul result from choosing to live by the coast. Tides govern time and travel plans; gorse blooms and storm clouds feel more vibrant with a sea breeze on your face. Living by the sea is said to make people happier and to me this is not a statistic, poll or science. The sea fills life with a deeper, brighter, more mouth-watering range of colours. The physical foundations of salt are vital to life and salt is my most important ingredient. Even the fine sandy coating on fish 'n' chips eaten on a bench outside the fish market is like no other for its ability to enhance and transform.

Simply put, all salt comes from the ocean. All salt is produced either directly from seawater or sourced from rock salt deposits formed from long-forgotten seas that have dried up and been compressed underground under vast tectonic pressure over millions of years. Salt is extracted either when seawater is evaporated into sea salt or by mining from ancient lakes as rock salt.

Salts in the ocean occur naturally from dissolved rocks and will have a different mineral composition depending on the geology along the coastline. This is what gives salts a distinctive regional terroir around the globe. Sodium bonded with chlorides (NaCl) is the most common form of salt found in natural brines and this naturally forms into a cuboid structure if immersed in solution. Other salts are made with different mineral compounds of elements, though they are always a metal and an acid joined together in solution with ionic bonds holding them together. They are then crystallised, as more water evaporates, into an array of solid salts as the brine concentrates. This crystallisation happens at slightly different times and levels of concentration, hence the stratification that can be seen in some rock salt as the salts in ancient seas crystallised at different stages of their evaporation. Seawater ranges from 3.2 per cent to 4 per cent salinity. Salt springs can be much higher – up to 33 per cent.

Most salt production around the world today is heavily standardised on a large scale. The process of making table salt removes almost all other minerals, leaving a product that's at least 99.8 per cent sodium chloride. Compare this to a good artisan sea salt, like the ones I use in this book, where the percentage of sodium chloride could be as low as 85 per cent and balanced with more than 60 beneficial sea minerals deliberately captured and laminated onto the crystals for more flavour and better balance – to me there's no competition when deciding which salt to choose to cook with.

Under the Microscope

Salt crystals are essentially two charged particles (in this case a metal, sodium, and an acid, chlorine). Also known as ions or electrolytes, they bond together to form a structure commonly described as a salt. There are eleven key ions in all salts and their presence is a good sign of a more naturally produced salt rather than a heavily refined version stripped down to only its essential parts of sodium and chloride.

Scientifically speaking, salt is an electrically neutral crystalline substance that is produced by the reaction of a base sodium and an acid chloride. Positive and negative charged ions bond to form a

(Above) Artic sea salt flakes

neutral compound. When dissolved in water, salt becomes an electrolyte that acts as electric pathways to conduct signals and convey information around the body. It is key to many bodily functions, such as water retention within our cells, and is a vital part of our diet.

Salts are made from dissolved rocks that all have their own unique geological mineral composition. Once dissolved into seawater, the rocks become charged salt ions floating in a solution and, when they are then evaporated out of a concentrated brine, they crystallise into solid salts that reflect the particular flavour and geological fabric of the coastline they originate from. When tasted, they reveal the varying levels of the minerals they contain: sodium, magnesium, calcium and potassium, according to the rocks in the local area. These subtle differences in minerals provide distinctive flavours that can be detected on our tongues when tasting one salt to the next. Higher levels of magnesium and calcium can be responsible for increased levels of sweetness in a salt, while potassium can provide a distinctive bitter flavour.

When I refer to salt in this book, I am referring to the edible salt primarily made up of 85–99.8 per cent sodium chloride rather than other salts such as magnesium sulphate or calcium chloride, and my goal is to broaden our understanding of salt to include more minerals like potassium, magnesium and calcium which naturally occur in a good sea salt. I want us to go beyond the combination of sodium and chloride that is responsible for so much of the bad press relating to health issues. Instead we should take a more balanced view that some salts which contain an array of sea minerals are better than others that are predominantly sodium chloride, for example, table salt.

How is Salt Made?

The production of salt can be broken down into:

Solar Salt – normally found in hot coastal areas where seawater is collected behind flood gates in

(*Above*) *Rose salt*

shallow salt pans at high tide and then concentrated in the sun to evaporate the water.

Fire Salt – heated until the water evaporates and a concentrated brine forms.

Rock Salt – mined salt that is either removed from underground as a solid and then milled and sold unprocessed, like Himalayan Pink salt, or salt that is dissolved underground to then be pumped to the surface for processing and turned into PDV (Pure Dried Vacuum) salt.

Vacuum-evaporated salts are made efficiently on a huge scale and are a cheap commodity with thousands of commercial uses, ranging from agriculture and pharmaceuticals to gritting roads and making soap. When the dissolved brine is heated, it releases steam and then the concentrated brine is transferred to large crystallisation tanks to be processed further. Brine is often sold in this liquid form for a number of food and beverage manufacturing applications and to the chemical and pharmaceutical industries. Brine provides the raw material to extract many chemicals such as chlorine, hydrogen and sodium using electrolysis.

To make table salt, all the other valuable sea minerals are stripped off as they emerge and start to crystallise in the brine and only pure sodium chloride salt crystals are allowed to form. These are then dried and coated in anti-caking agents. Many of the other salts that are removed are particularly hygroscopic, which means they attract water, and this makes them difficult to process. PDV (Pure Dried Vacuum) salt is designed to be dry and free-flowing but devoid of any complex sea minerals. It's functional rather than flavoursome.

To make good sea salts, however, the flakes are deliberately harvested slowly to allow more sea minerals to coat them as the brine concentrates. As more of the water in the brine evaporates, crystallisation occurs naturally. This is because there is not enough water to hold the salt-forming ions in solution, so they bond together into crystals.

This stage is known as primary nucleation. A seed forms in the solution first and then, at the second stage, the remaining ions in the concentrated brine attract one another more than the water around them, so they form into tiny crystals that build and build on the initial seed crystal. Stirring the brine at the point of second nucleation agitates it and helps form larger crystals and beautiful architectural flakes. Open-air brine tanks sited on the coast will shimmer with the wind and this can naturally help with crystal formation. There's a salt-makers' belief that *Halobacterium salinarum* present in some seawater may also help form a seed crystal. These are a type of harmless salt-loving bacterium that thrive in areas of high salt concentration and provide an anchor for the seed crystals to form. Eventually the salt flakes and crystals are rinsed in the concentrated brine, also known as bittern, to clean them while also simultaneously laminating them with more valuable, hygroscopic (water-loving) salts. Once they are shiny, they are then dried before packing to be sold.

Salt making can be very variable, dependent not only on the local climate but also the seasons. For example, seashells extract calcium and grow quicker in the summer than in the winter, so you will find more calcium in salts made with winter seawaters.

(Above) Fleur de Sel

How Salt Crystals Grow

Mineral-rich salt flakes grow as upside-down pyramids suspended on the surface of the crystallisation tanks. They hang there until they break the surface tension and float slowly to the bottom. The sodium chloride crystals form around a tiny seed so the charged ions are in balance – this is why they form equally at right angles. The pure sodium chloride crystal is cuboid and square-shaped but, as it develops, a pyramidal structure emerges – layers of sodium chloride and other minerals bond to the charged surface. So, as each layer bonds and gets heavier, the newly formed salt crystals sink. This all happens half a millimetre at a time and the process repeats along each four surface angles.

When you look through a microscope, you can see the inverted pyramids, sometimes called hopper crystals due to their shape. Although there are geometric shapes to natural sea salt, look closer and each flake should be unique, bearing a mineral and crystalline imprint that indicates the elemental and human forces that made it.

Hold some salt in the palm of your hand and you should see a chaotic, fractal world of pyramids and broken shards – this lets you know it contains the good stuff, a mix of sea minerals laminated to the crystal. Sadly, most salt you will still find today has been homogenised into the cuboid, minerally-deficient table salt that lacks any character and is difficult for our bodies to process. Nowhere on Earth does pure sodium chloride occur naturally – we are simply not designed to consume it.

Making Salt

Have a go at making your own sea salt at home from a couple of litres of seawater collected from a local beach. This is a great science experience for children to witness and, if you take your time, you can yield about 20–30g/¾–1oz of salt from 2 litres/3½ pints of seawater.

1. Collect some clean seawater. In the UK, seawater is graded on how clean it is – often to indicate

whether shellfish can be consumed raw or need processing. Avoid seawater where there is an effluent pipe nearby or adjacent farmland where there may be pesticide or animal waste run-off. Use some common sense and research how clean your local seawater is before harvesting it to make salt – if in doubt, contact your local council authority for advice.

2. After collecting, allow the seawater to settle for an hour. Leave the dregs and sediment to fall to the bottom and then siphon or carefully pour off the clean-looking seawater above. Next, filter it twice through a sieve lined with a double layer of cheesecloth or muslin.

3. Pour the filtered seawater into a heavy-based, stainless steel pan and simmer over a medium heat for 10 hours or at a low simmer for at least 15 hours until it evaporates. Simmer at least half of the water off and then make sure you turn the heat right down. A few bubbles on the surface are okay but keep it at a low simmer. An extraction fan can help while evaporating the water to reduce the humidity in the kitchen and therefore make it easier for the seawater to concentrate as steam evaporates off the surface.

4. After 10–15 hours, when the seawater has reduced so that only one third of the original volume remains, turn up the heat. Do not shake or stir and don't let the pan boil dry.

5. Salt will form in the saucepan and, as the salt crystals get bigger, some may sink. When only a few millimetres of water remain, the sea salt crystals are ready to harvest. Lift them out carefully with a spoon and place on a sheet of kitchen paper or a clean kitchen towel. Once all the sea salt crystals have been removed, scrape down the side of the pan and discard this – these are probably calcium salts (which are edible but not really what you are after to cook with as they taste unpleasantly bitter).

6. Leave the harvested sea salt crystals to dry for a few minutes and then carefully spread them out on a baking sheet in a dehydrator (at 50–75°C/122–167°F) or on a baking parchment-lined baking tray in a preheated oven (at 50–75°C fan/158–203°F/very low gas oven) to dry fully before storing. They should be dry within 1–2 hours. Cool, then store in a sealed jar for as long as the crystals remain dry. Salt can be kept indefinitely, as it is an inorganic compound that doesn't degrade, so how long it lasts is down to keeping it dry rather than a conventional shelf life.

Chapter Two
Types of Salt

There are many different salts from around the world and in order to understand how to use them you need to look closely at their pyramidal structure, understand a little more about the crystallisation process and appreciate how mineral lamination impacts on flavour.

Principally, there are PDV (Pure Dried Vacuum) table salts (which are mass produced and heavily processed sea salts that are sourced from seawater but tend to be stripped of everything except sodium chloride before they reach our kitchens) and rock salts, but there are also a huge number of other regional river and sea salts, all with their own distinctive shape and flavour, such as *fleur de sel* and *sel gris*, and kosher and lava salt.

Before we really delve into the salts out there, let's address the elephant in the room. Table salt is not the same as sea salt or a good rock salt. Table salt is only good for gritting pathways or using to make salt dough for children to play with. To put it bluntly – table salt is not for eating. I do not own any table salt and don't use it to cook with ever. I prefer the flavour and depth from good salt rather than a one-dimensional chemical tang from table salt.

The heavily refined salt you will find in table salt is almost 99.8 per cent sodium chloride as opposed to a mineral-rich sea salt that can be as low as 85 per cent sodium chloride. To me, it only provides a monotone, binary type of seasoning that to a seasoned chef is blasphemy. Personally, I don't even use table salt for pasta or vegetable cooking water. A natural sea salt contains 60+ beneficial sea minerals, all driving flavour together to enliven more parts of the palate and heighten our experience of eating by conveying messages across multiple pathways. The ingenuity of people around the world to produce gourmet, artisan salts in myriad ways astounds me. Be adventurous and try lots of the different salts out there until you start to learn how best to use them in your kitchen.

The Shape of Salt

Sea salt flakes are salts that have been grown on the surface of the brine. In many cultures, especially in areas of northern France, where the temperate climate is on the edge of feasibility for making solar salts, this flower of the salt – the ornate seed crystal that forms into flakes like crystalline petals – is highly valued and in natural salinas only occurs at certain times of the brine cycle when the weather conditions are perfect. For example, a lunar tide flooding the salt pans when a perfectly balanced zephyr combines with the right temperatures from the sun. There is a lot of secrecy in the salt-making world because the art (or science) of growing these crystals suspended from the surface of the brine while still having the complex of minerals takes time to perfect – it is an extremely temperamental process which is hugely affected by the weather, temperature of the brine and local salinity.

The gourmet salt market prefers flat platelet flake salt or hollow pyramid-shaped crystal structures compared to a cuboid sodium chloride crystals such as table salt. The look and feel of these gourmet salts has more appeal among chefs and foodies for finishing, but flakes and hollow crystals also have a big functional advantage for cooking. These lighter forms of crystal structure have a much larger surface area and lower structural density, so they dissolve rapidly in contact with water or on your tongue. Quick dissolution provides waves of flavour across your taste buds to instantly convey taste while the food is in your mouth. By contrast, a rock salt on something like a pretzel that hits your tongue for a moment but needs chewing and crunching to break down will only provide limited bursts of flavour and then dissolve in your gut without the benefit of providing taste.

The other big, but lesser-known advantage is that in sea salt production this expansive inverted pyramid structure can also act as a platform for other minerals that are still in solution to coat or laminate the surface of the flake. The addition of these other minerals is not only an advantage for flavour balance but also means that it is possible for many other essential electrolytes, including calcium, magnesium and potassium, to be present on the surface of the crystal. These essential minerals, plus trace elements such as zinc, boron, iron and phosphorous are vital for our bodies – mineral deficiencies can have as damaging long-term consequences as too much sodium. Rather than buying magnesium or potassium supplements from a health food shop, doesn't it make more sense to choose a salt that contains the minerals we need?

This is also the case for some more dense crystal structures harvested from naturally occurring rock salt but not to the same proportion as sea salt due to the structural density and distinct stratification of rock salt, as it often forms in pronounced layers of various salt deposits.

The Many Tastes of Salt

The flavour of salt itself can taste like the summer sea, briny bittersweet, or leave you with a sulphuric metallic tang. As soon as you start to think differently about sea salt, not as a single entity devoid of character but instead like individuals in a charming seaside village story, each one unique and with its own foodie culture, you will see that no good salt tastes the same. Noticing the subtle differences is a real start towards appreciation and changing the way you cook.

My whole approach to food is focused on local, seasonal and organic food, so it probably goes without saying that I'm much more interested in artisan

salts than industrial scaled products. I will cover some mined rock salts due to their unique mineral composition, colour or flavour, but primarily, I want to shine a light on smaller-scale salt manufacturers and non-mechanised production methods where the crystallisation tanks are carefully raked by hand to harvest the salts, producing high-quality ingredients. The correlation between using local and seasonal ingredients seasoned with an artisan salt makes so much sense. They go together seamlessly well.

Later in this book, I will put on my sommelier hat and talk you through how I approach choosing the right salt for a particular recipe. It's not an exact science and I'm sure that you will combine your own favourite partnerships, but artisan salt is as impactful, if not more so, than choosing the right wine to accompany a menu. Try to perceive artisan salts in the same way we now acknowledge craft beer or a micro distillery. Fortunately, there are more and more micro-salt producers springing up around the coast and I hope it's a trend that continues to grow.

(Left) Red wine and white wine salt
(Above) Whiskey salt

Salts from around the world with their own unique flavours are like spices to a chef, with infinite variety and impact. They genuinely can elevate food.

Heritage Revival

As mining technology advanced over the last few hundred years, many smaller saltworks closed. It became cheaper and more efficient to mine for rock salt that was then ground up or to dissolve the huge beds of solid salt underground into a brine, pump that to the surface and vacuum-evaporate it into the refined salt we know today.

Luckily some old-fashioned methods of salt production, the peculiar, spectacular and ingenious, have survived the tests of time or are enjoying a revival. What I love about what I see today is that the old artisan salt production methods are being brought back to life.

Japan, as always, was ahead of the curve. Before provenance became a buzzword, they'd reconnected to their artisan traditions and focused on mineral balance and complex processes to create special, delicious salts. Micro salt-making businesses provide a thriving salt culture in Japan, to my knowledge only rivalled by the large array of distinctive rectangular salt pans or salinas of the kind found near Aveiro along the coast of Portugal.

In Scotland, there is a favourite salt of mine where the brine is concentrated on giant blackthorn hedges where the seawater is evaporated by the wild North Sea breeze. In the Nordic region, a number of salt producers are using warm waters from naturally occurring geothermal springs to concentrate their brine before crystallisation, and in France, the *paludiers* are making *fleur de sel* in nearly the same way they have been for hundreds of years. It's impossible to guess what is next for salt, but I hope that there is a return to these smaller-scale saltworks rather than the continued reliance on larger scale, heavily-processed cheap salts.

Organic Salt

For me this is a conflict in terms as, by nature, salt is a non-organic compound that contains no living parts of plants or animals, so surely can't be classified as organic. Instead of considering a purchase based on an organic status, I suggest looking for salts that come from clean waters and environmentally-aware companies who are trying to incorporate sustainable procedures into their manufacturing.

Where to Find Salt?

Many retailers and delis now stock a range of salts. Provenance has become so important to cooks that there are more ways to buy good salts. I try to support traditional local economies and artisans rather than big business. So, it's with great excitement I've been witnessing the vast variety of artisan salt makers emerging around the UK. Artisan salt makers are regaining ground lost to industrial manufacturers. The innovative spirit is dazzling, and constant tinkering with the process, tasting brines and perfecting evaporation techniques has given rise to more and more salts being produced for us to try.

I have been able to buy so many salts online and there are major salt merchants, distributors and importers who select a good mix of larger salt producers and smaller more niche varieties. For me, salt is the new holiday souvenir or the replacement for a bottle of wine to take round to a friend's house as a gift, but also remember to look close to home and see where your nearest salt producer is based.

Solar Salt

Made directly from seawater in oceans, lakes, tidal rivers or briny springs, solar salt requires a dry, temperate climate and is normally made in hot weather for best results. The method can be employed in the open air, in a greenhouse or in a polytunnel but relies on the sun to evaporate water and concentrate the brine to eventually form sea salt.

Some famous types of solar salt include *fleur de sel*, *sel gris*, sea salt flakes and traditional crystals. The mineral composition of solar salts tends to include a good mixture of sea minerals and deliver complex flavour; they therefore also naturally contain a lower percentage of sodium.

(Above) Sea salt flakes
(Right) Fleur de sel

Fleur de Sel

Fleur de sel has been made in France using similar artisan techniques for hundreds of years. Like many of the great French culinary success stories, they own the space with a degree of pride that verges on condemnation for anything other than their own ingredients. I respect this celebration of an engrained local food tradition, but you will also find many other wonderful salts made in a similar fashion elsewhere without the label of *fleur de sel*. Much like French champagne, where it is now accepted that even the English make a tasty sparkling wine, so it is with salts from Spain, Portugal, Italy and all around the globe.

With *fleur de sel*, there is very little to no magnesium as the salts are raked and harvested from shallow pans outside before the magnesium salts form. The process is hugely labour-intensive but worth it for the silvery pink-coloured flakes. They are fine and delicate, carefully skimmed off the surface and scraped from the shallow pan without disturbing the grey porcelain clay at the bottom and ruining the *fleur de sel* by tainting the colour.

The salt must be harvested in the afternoon before it settles to the bottom of the cooler salt pans where the newly formed crystals absorb grey clay minerals and so are transformed into *sel gris*. Every moment counts for the *paludiers* or salt workers; timing is everything. This makes it the ultimate micro-seasonal salt, dependent on the warm weather conditions and local climate, with the wind also playing a key role in aiding evaporation across the ponds. It is highly irregular and the fine crystals have a moderate level of residual moisture – because of this, they resist dissolving immediately when put on food, so you get a lovely crunch when eating.

Fleur de sel is highly satisfying to use as the large flakes provide an intense surge of salinity that's then followed by a wave of flavour as the smaller flakes dissolve fast into solution in your saliva to wash your mouth with another blast of flavour. The complex blend of trace minerals deepens flavour and it really is one of the ultimate finishing salts.

(*Above and right*) *Sel gris*

Sel Gris

Also known as bay salt or sometimes *gros gris* salt – which is the extra crunchy type – this grey salt is made by traditional methods and requires a combination of vigilance and hard work from the *paludiers* to harvest. I find it a truly romantic salt that conjures up the picture of a zephyr cast across the shimmering *oeillet*, or harvesting ponds, surrounded by salt marshes, breathing life into a bloom of salt on the silvery surface. Once the *fleur de sel* has been harvested, the coarser, moister crystals form on the top of the salt pans but drop down to the bottom as they break the surface tension of the brine. Shovelling these crystals is a fine balance to get right. The greyness of *sel gris* varies greatly but is a key part of its rustic appeal. This colouring is a part of the character and tradition, but too much dark clay colour makes it look unappealing and dirty. The benefit though is a serious mineral depth of flavour and a hearty crunch.

It takes a fair amount of confidence and attitude to use *sel gris* at the right time in the kitchen – mixed with a certain dash of French flair. For me, this salt translates well as grey salt because it needs some maturity to handle it in the right way. The silvery bite is superb for cooking with but not for curing or rubs and personally I don't like using it as a finishing salt. As it's already high in moisture, *sel gris* is less effective at osmosis and doesn't dissolve quickly when in contact with food.

Crystals

This is a magnificent type of salt, sometimes simply referred to as traditional salt. The crystals that I like to use are crunchy and coarse, so much so that often they need grinding to use. Usually, crystals are the result of solar salts that are harvested once or twice a year if produced outside or made in heated salt tanks where they are commercially produced on a more efficient scale. Salt crystals are rocky, crunchy but very tasty. The crust of traditional salts that crystallise in the brine is rich in trace minerals and this is sometimes called the cake. It can be thick and raked by hand or, on a larger scale, mechanical help is used, even by some artisan producers. The slowly formed crystals can be haphazard chunks or perfect blocks built like a pyramid under construction but less geometric than salt flakes. Crystals can be ground into shards, finely milled or kept coarse for texture. This is my go-to salt for cooking, as it's functional, tasty and easy to use. I always keep a pot of salt crystals next to the oven when cooking and use it whenever I want texture as well as seasoning in a dish.

Flakes

Sea salt flakes are the sexy salt that steals the show. They look like frozen sculptures or an ocean freezing over. Through a macro lens or microscope, flakes are spellbinding. Available to buy as fine flakes or super large flakes, they are sharp-edged with defined shapes like inverted hollow boxes. Their huge surface area means they dissolve quickly on the tongue and the visual impact means they lend themselves to finishing a dish with some pizzazz. When you taste a sea salt flake, it's like an electric jolt on your tongue.

Salt flakes are illuminating. They are produced by a host of secretive and diverse methods around the world. Everything makes a difference to the end flake – water temperature, rate of evaporation, salinity, and the process of stirring at second nucleation to form their shape and size. When I get my tattoo of salt (probably as a celebration of this book), it will almost definitely be of an iconic salt flake.

Fire Evaporation

This type of salt, evaporated by fire and generated heat, comes from the same source of seawater as solar salt – oceans, lakes and springs – but normally in cooler areas that are more rainy and less sunny. Often there's a degree of solar salt-making to kickstart the process before heating. The production process will normally be housed in a greenhouse or a large polytunnel first to make the necessary concentrated brine; it is then crystallised in a large vat or cauldron over fire.

For this process, a concentrated brine is heated over a fire that's fed slowly for a better crystallisation. On the Lizard Peninsula here in Cornwall, remnants have been found of Roman clay pots where salt was made under gorse fires. The source of heat is evolving with some Scandinavian salt-producers using geothermal technology, while others are replacing fire with electrolysis to facilitate ion separation, the part of the process where the bonded ions and compounds split when an electric current is passed through the solvent, in this case, seawater, so that the dissolved ions are available for salt making.

Shio

The most famous type of fire-evaporated salt is shio. While rapid boiling produces layered parchment-like, pyramidal flakes, slower simmering produces shio – a fine-grained sea salt mastered by Japanese salt makers and the most delicate crystals you will find. The brine is rich and saturated with magnesium, so with the perfect amount of agitation at key stages of production and a dash of Japanese precision, a bloom of tiny crystals forms. When

(Above) Sea salt flakes

the salts are agitated, it induces small tufts of fine salt like dandelion seeds floating in the bittern. A handful of artisans then form this precious salt into moulds to create a dried puck of shio salt – it is on my bucket list to watch this magic in action. The microscopic flakes are like bittersweet magnesium confetti to season. The perfect salt to sprinkle on dry foods like popcorn or edamame. Cooking with shio is like sprinkling soft snowflakes that fall onto open-mouthed tongues to dissolve with Zen-like mastery. Subtlety that reminds us that heritage techniques still cater to the most modern and sophisticated tastes.

Rock Salt

My love affair with rock salt fluctuates from day to day. Sometimes, I will rave about the miraculous flavour from a stunning piece of rock salt, marvelling at the gemstone colours and carved surfaces. At other times, I will feel quietly ashamed by the environmental impact of using it because the mining process often relies on heavy machinery, noisy blasting and unsafe working conditions.

Rock salt comprises one third of global salt production. Another third is produced as brine, and the remainder as PDV (Pure Dried Vacuum) salt, fire salt and, finally, solar sea salt. Rock salt is made from dried-up seas formed a few million to hundreds of millions of years ago. They are often huge monolithic crystals underground and contain no moisture. They are found as either bedded salt, not very deep but spread out in horizontal beds beneath the surface, or occasionally salt domes rising from the surface. Sometimes the rock beds are so near the surface they result in briny ponds or salt licks. Animal tracks leading to salt licks have even given rise to human settlements following their prey – Buffalo City in the United States is said to have been built at the end of a well-trodden salt lick path.

Rock salt is usually quarried and is also called *halite*. Mined from great deposits underground, the calcium salts crystallise at the top, with a massive middle layer of primarily sodium chloride, and lastly,

(Above) Japanese shio

magnesium and potassium salts that crystallise more slowly and therefore lie deeper underground. The mining process is fuel hungry with lots of specialist equipment, explosives and commercial grinding. Only a small percentage of rock salt is used for food salts and it is very common for water to be pumped underground into rock salt deposits to make a dissolved brine, which is then pumped up to the surface where it is vacuum evaporated and refined to form 99.8 per cent sodium chloride. This is how most table salt is produced.

Rock salt's gemstone-like lumps truly do have an otherworldly beauty but must be dissolved or ground to make them edible. Rock salt is sold in many forms and can be grated superfine with a rock salt shaver, added to a mill to grind at the table or carved into salt blocks to cook with.

The origins of rock salt don't tell you much about the actual salt you cook with. Often you can't depend on a wide mineral mix, but you can often get coloured salts from impurities in the salt – iron oxide, for example, is what gives Himalayan Pink salt its colour. As a type of salt, Himalayan Pink is functional and can easily be ground for a small, fine grain that's good for an even coverage.

(*Above*) *Rock salt*

paying more money for it in a shop. Kosher salt can be entirely refined or be a natural sea salt. Look closely at the crystals or research where it comes from before buying on faith alone. Often recipes will refer to Kosher salt because they think that the name means it is tastier, but look for Kosher salt that's been made from natural sea salt or a minerally-complex rock salt that's been koshered.

Table Salt

Table salt is a refined salt that can either come from sea salt or rock salt, and it has had most of the moisture taken out of it. This makes table salt very thirsty, or hygroscopic, so the salt wants to attract water and, if left alone, it would clump together, so anti-caking agents are added. These aluminium-based compounds have been shown to be bad for your health but are also more difficult for your body to process.

Kosher Salt

Kosher actually relates to the food-handling conformance or *kashrut* in Jewish dietary law, not directly to the type of salt. It has nothing to do with health or quality, so don't be confused by this when

Bittern

This is the sodium-depleted brine that remains after salt is made. Known as *nigari* in Japan – the word stems from the Japanese term for bitter – it's so much more than a by-product, full of mineral compounds with enormous flavour and cooking application. The salts in bittern are very water-soluble and hygroscopic, which means they attract water, so it normally comes supplied as a liquid or paste. That said, you can buy *nigari* flakes or magnesium chloride salts easily online and some salt manufacturers are now starting to sell bittern as a bottled liquid for lower sodium seasoning. With many health benefits and because it is rich in magnesium chloride and magnesium sulphate, it is popular in beauty products. Bittern is also used as a coagulant for plant proteins like tofu.

Chapter Three
A Pinch of History

Salt helped early civilisations adapt beyond groups of nomadic hunter-gatherers, who would get their bodily salt requirements from meat, into agricultural communities who could preserve food all year round. As far back as the ancient Egyptians around 6,500 BC and over 6,000 years ago in ancient China, people have developed systems for salt production and used salt to reduce our dependence on seasonal food. With salt, we developed the ability to transport food over great distances, allowing us to explore the world and build empires. People have always risen to the challenge to expand and make or mine salt all around the world. In my view, our determined imagination to produce salt has been a significant factor in exploration. It could be argued that salt was one of the pivotal foods that shaped civilisation.

In Europe, salt has always been instrumental to growth and trade. The major sea salt producers started in the Mediterranean. The Romans and Venetians set up saltworks and used their monopolies to increase their political dominance. Establishing an empire is not solely attributable to the availability of salt, but it certainly helped. The Romans required salt for their army and horses, so they set up more than 60 saltworks around the Roman empire. The *Via Salaria* or Salt Road that led from Rome 242km or 150 miles to the Adriatic coast was one of the very first great Roman roads. This approach of strategically located and productive saltworks linked to empire building endured for thousands of years. In Britain, towns ending with a *–wich* denote old saltworks, for example, Nantwich and Droitwich.

As their empires eventually declined, there was a shift towards the Atlantic salt producers who grew to prominence. Salt made in Portugal, Britain, Holland and France fuelled the exploration of the Americas in the 1500s and 1600s. As colonial North America was establishing itself, salt was produced on Caribbean islands throughout the seventeenth and eighteenth centuries, often subject to piracy and conflict over control. But then saltworks started to spring up along the East coast of the United States in the 1860s in response to rising prices from Britain and to reduce the huge volume of heavily taxed imports. They produced huge amounts of salt and eventually secured autonomy to reduce their reliance on salt from Europe.

A Sign of Status

Historically, salt cellars on the table were an ornate status symbol. How near you sat to the salt at the table was an indicator of social standing. In poorer households, salt would have been simply displayed in a seashell.

I think that we are not so different today to people from the past. In fact, the way we use and display salt still indicates status, wealth and style. Today, we may choose to display a ceramic salt pig rimming with artisan salt flakes in a prime position next to the oven, or we may have a fancy rock salt grinder to adorn the table.

Salt's Symbolic Value

The word 'salary' comes from the Latin *sal* meaning salt. It is reputed Roman legionaries were paid in salt or were at least seen to be 'worth their salt'. This notion of value associated with salt has become embedded in our language. The French word *solde*, also stemming from *sal*, meaning pay, is also where the English word 'soldier' originates from.

Historically, salt was also regularly used to bind agreements. There are numerous examples of symbolic wedding gifts involving salt to seal pacts. Israel, Syria and Egypt used salt as part of greetings, celebrations and agreements, a tradition to exchange a pinch of salt from one pouch to another. Supposedly, the deal couldn't be broken unless they could retrieve their own grains of salt from the other partner's pouch. In medieval Britain, salt was used as well as gold for trade deals.

Praising someone by referring to them as 'salt of the earth' stems from a biblical phrase that has come to mean humble, hard-working and kind. It's also a mark of honesty and good character to be 'worth their salt'.

Controlling the salt is something that every chef understands – we understand the power of salt.

This is why in a restaurant the salt will normally be in a bowl on the pass next to the chef. Historically, it has been pretty similar with imperial nations, colonialists and despots all monopolising the salt. Every so often, there have been salt rebellions, none more famous than in India. Mohandas Gandhi was fuelled by the British salt monopoly of the time to gain independence. Gandhi and his followers walked the 240 miles to the sea to break the law and harvest their own salt in protest at the British policy. What started out as a dozen people turned into thousands and in 1931 the Indian people won the right to collect their own salt. To seal the deal, Gandhi was offered a cup of tea from the Viceroy of India as an olive branch and attempt at appeasement. He famously refused and instead asked for water, lemon and a pinch of salt.

Finally, salt is sexy. The Romans called a man in lust *salax* – being in a salted state is the origin of the word 'salacious'. In Spain, bridal couples went to church with salt in their left pocket to guard against impotency, while in Germany, the bride's shoes were sprinkled with salt.

———

An Essential Element

We have about 250g or 9oz of salt in our bodies. It is essential for us to survive, helps us retain water within our cells and conveys messages to our brains when dissolved into electrolytes. Meat is a natural source of salt whereas vegetables aren't. This is part of the reason why hunter-gatherers in North America neither made nor traded for salt while agricultural peoples did.

Interestingly, Masai nomadic cattle herders meet their salt requirements by bleeding livestock and drinking the blood. I'm not suggesting a return to relying on meat for our salt requirements, but

I do find it fascinating to think how much our relationship with salt has changed and how there might be a risk of becoming minerally deficient by adopting a plant-based diet. By removing meat and fish from your diet, you may need to increase your salt intake by adding more to your vegetables. Wild herbivores actively forage for salt. If you were to follow an array of animal tracks in the wild, they would often lead to a natural salt lick or brine spring.

Preservation

Pre-refrigeration, livestock was often slaughtered in winter and salted to preserve the meat when fodder crops were in scarce supply. The role of salt to preserve foods is enormous and has played a huge part in the supply and demand of food and movement of people. Garum sauces that are salty, fish-based ferments were extremely popular at the time of the Roman and Venetian empire but fell out of favour due to the intensity of their taste and aroma. Recently though, I've noticed a resurgence of interest in fermented salted fish and predict that more and more restaurants will soon be producing umami-rich, salty garum sauce to elevate their menus.

In the past, salt was a ticket to travel. If food could be preserved, then longer voyages and exploration became possible. Salt pork and beef played a huge role in transporting food at the time of maritime exploration and colonialism. Salted fish was also hugely popular in Europe when the Christian calendar was peppered with fasts. The landing and curing in salt of both herring and then cod were a way to circumvent the fasts with protein when meat was off the table.

Salt Today

There are hundreds of uses for salt today and the modern salt industry claims that there are more than 14,000 wide-ranging applications, including pharmaceuticals, melting ice on roads, making soap, various uses in the textile industry, multiple agricultural roles and, most importantly to me, the preparation and cooking of food.

Historically, salt was used primarily to preserve food, and for those few people who could afford it, to enhance its flavour. The huge growth in how it's used today has made salt a victim of its own success. In our desire to produce more salt, we've started using the same product in our food that we use to grit our roads. It's incredible how useful salt is across many industries, but for cooking we need to take a step back in time and return to using more naturally produced salts full of tasty minerals. We need to stop eating refined table salt just because it's cheaper and look after our health by consuming salt that's naturally lower in sodium.

Chapter Four
Friend or Foe?

Salt is a subject of intense debate among health professionals, nutritionists and food writers and it's important for me to say that I'm not a nutritionist or a doctor. But what I am is informed about how my body works and responds to good food. Salt is crucial to our bodily functions and so is an understanding of how to use it properly. Sodium and potassium are vital to send messages to the brain and key for water absorption in our cells. Our electrolyte balance is a bit like voltage. Yet there's no way of storing the electrical current derived from salts in our bodies. We have a current that flows with salts which needs topping up rather than being retained in a battery.

I'm very lucky to be able to cook from scratch for myself and my family, almost all the time. This means I can choose how and when I add good natural salts to our diet. Natural salts aren't solely made with sodium chloride but instead contain other minerals that we need to survive, but sodium levels in food do matter. Too much sodium is very bad for your health, so even too much of a good thing can do you damage. The crux of the issue for me is that by using a tasty salt, which also happens to be naturally lower in sodium because it contains other necessary minerals, you can use less salt when cooking to season your food more effectively. This is because it tastes due to the mineral notes when dissolved on your palate, so even with less salt you can deliver more flavour.

I work with many food manufactures in the UK who seek to reduce salt in their products and menus, until they understand that it's the percentage of sodium in the incumbent salt that they use for their production (normally a cheap table salt) which is the problem rather than just how much salt is in their recipes. A good sea salt will have a blend of other minerals laminating the flakes that automatically reduces the amount of sodium while continuing to boost flavour and provide beneficial sea minerals for your body. In fact, if you are doing this and are using mineral-rich, tasty salts, then you need to use far less than if cooking with horrible-tasting table salt that's extra bad for you with higher sodium levels.

The problem we are told is that too much salt leads to high blood pressure or hypertension and increases the risk of heart disease. Recent studies have shown people living within 1km of the coast are thought to be happier and perhaps sea salt has a role to play here. Salt water certainly seems to help your body heal and the salts can be absorbed into your skin, keeping it healthy, hydrated and increasing elasticity. Also, despite high levels of salt consumption, some Mediterranean countries still have a lower rate of heart disease than countries that consume less salt. This is in part probably down to climate, an enviable lifestyle and a good diet, but also because the salt they are eating more of is natural sea salt when they cook from scratch, rather than refined salts hidden in processed foods. The lethal combination is lots of 99.8 per cent sodium chloride table salt being used in processed foods without our knowledge. The food itself is often not even that tasty, so is it really worth it?

These hidden salts have been clamped down on by retailers and some multi-site restaurants, and traffic-light systems are in place in the UK to guide consumers safely away from really salty foods. But there is a distinction between salt as a problem and good salts being essential for mineral balance and health within our bodies, as they provide much-needed calcium, magnesium and potassium. For as long as the debate is solely focused, homogenously lumping all salts together as the bad guy, we will fail to understand the reality.

How Salt Affects Taste

At the beginning of this book, I suggested taking the tomato test to start to understand how taste works when you add salt. Salt amplifies the flavour compounds of food and when dissolved in your saliva allows information to be passed to your brain and shape your experience.

The more salt you add, the more pathways are available to transfer that info. The more minerals that are present in the salt, the more complex the message can become. Using table salt with just sodium chloride only allows a binary, singular taste experience. The result is one-dimensional. Alternatively, if you are tasting with a mineral-rich salt, then magnesium, calcium and potassium all play an important role in adjusting the intensity.

I find salts with a robust sea mineral profile enhance sweetness and leave pronounced bitter notes that mix up the flavour with sharper peaks and troughs and a resonant lightness. They still amplify the primary taste but simultaneously pump up other notes. However, to turn up the volume on your food, you can add less of a good salt to achieve more flavour than using more of a bad table salt – by up to 30 per cent – while still delivering the same, if not more, flavour. This is a massive health advantage, seasoning with good sea salt versus table salt – i.e. using less salt to deliver more flavour. To taste the difference first-hand, take the tomato test again and see what subtle disparities you detect.

Consider salt as a way to feed your body holistically with a natural diet of minerals that we need to thrive. I like to talk about salt in a similar fashion to real bread. For example, a loaf of sourdough will provide a mix of beneficial bacteria and wild yeasts that taste great and simultaneously aid digestion and boost our gut flora. Compared to a heavily refined white loaf made with standardised brewer's yeast, there is no contest which bread is going to be better for you. The same goes for salts – if they have a balance of sea minerals laminated on the flakes instead of being solely comprised of sodium chloride, then they will be better for your health and be tastier. Potassium, for example, naturally occurs with sodium and helps to reduce blood pressure. Consuming the right amount of good natural sea salts – containing these beneficial and essential minerals – is an excellent way to help balance your diet.

Taking Back Control

Sadly, food has moved away from home cooking, meaning that many of us have forgotten the place salt used to hold in our homes. Salting has become vague, strange and abstract. We have all become guilty of being too far removed from that most comfortable of actions: adding a pinch or a dash of salt when cooking at home. We have been made to doubt ourselves, and out of fears for our health, we've sacrificed tasty food for bland. Instead, our salt is managed and distributed by huge factories using enormous silos, full of finely milled mineral-depleted salt that is then hidden in our food. Seventy-five per cent of our salt comes from prepared or processed foods. So, cook from scratch for better-seasoned food that you can control. Cook and eat intelligently and look before you buy. Ask questions and become radicalised.

A Quick Guide to Buying Healthier Salt

Look for natural sea salt – there are often visual clues, as the crystals will appear messy, organic and not uniform. This means they contain more than pure sodium chloride.

Buy local – find your local sea salt manufacturer and support them. Traditional salt economies and smaller producers often make salt that is easier for your body to process. Encouraging the emergence of more micro-salt manufacturing by choosing to shop local first will help stimulate a greater understanding of our *merroir* and celebrate the different salts from around the coastline.

Throw away your cheap table salt and get rid of any industrial salts like cheap refined sea salt or processed kosher salt – use them to grit your path in the winter. They're also pretty good at deterring slugs from salad beds in the summer.

Ask what the mineral profile of salt is and seek out salt that is rich in calcium, magnesium or potassium. The quantities are tiny, almost indiscernible, but a salt with a richer mineral profile is better for your health.

(Right) Sea salt flakes

How to Season

Part Two

Chapter Five
The Science of Taste

From a salt perspective, it's evident that we evolved from the sea because the same 21 essential minerals in our bodies exactly match those in the sea and, remarkably, in the same quantities. These minerals all occur in perfect balance in sea salt and they are not only important for health, but they also facilitate enhanced taste. Our saliva has 1 per cent salinity, so when we add salt to food, we allow additional connections from the dissolved acids and metals to convey information from the food to our taste buds. This transfer of information amplifies flavour, and the more sea minerals in our salt, the more intense our understanding of taste.

The reason I don't want to get too caught up on taste as a pure science is that cooking in a kitchen is not like working in a lab. Food is not lines of Petri dishes containing pure substances, it's a mixture of ingredients. We can learn much about the functionality of salt as a taste, but keep that instinctive side with your cooking and listen to the small whispers from food guiding you on how to adjust flavour as you cook. Your job as a seasoned cook is to taste and then choose to add more salt or not. Repeat this several times whenever you cook. A deftness of hand to adjust the seasoning little by little also makes all the difference, so make sure you practise your salt pinch skills.

Flavour vs Taste

Taste and flavour are terms that are often blurred and used interchangeably, but they are distinct from one another. There are five tastes: sweet, sour, salty, bitter and umami (savoury). As a chef, working with tastes is like an artist in their studio working with primary colours. The chemical compounds are like the paints that illustrate an ingredient. To me, flavour is how the combination of tastes come together in a recipe, and the way we interpret or describe this combination. Flavour is a painting that we describe with words, and taste is the palette. You

(Left) An umami flavour bomb – truffle salt seasoning some sautéed mushrooms with garlic and thyme. Served on toast, there aren't many things tastier to eat for breakfast.

can blend individual tastes like bitter and sweet, salty and umami into unique and vibrant secondary and complementary colour combinations. Salt is connected to all of these in the way it interacts and changes their potency. For me, salt is the taste that makes the most difference to the levels of flavour itself. It is the captain of the ship, the seasoned helmsman sailing us to a tasty destination.

Bitter and Sour

Bitterness and sour flavours originally existed to warn us of potentially harmful foods and the possibility of toxins. Salt reduces bitterness. If you don't believe me, take a simple tonic test. Pour yourself two glasses of tonic water. Place a pinch of salt into one and stir it. Taste the unsalted tonic and experience that slight bitterness that lingers on your palate. Now try the salted tonic. You will find it tastes less bitter, even sweet by comparison. The salt dials down the bitter taste. This ability to play with other core tastes is used across so much cookery. I always add a pinch of salt to bitter dark chocolate or to a grapefruit salad. Bitter foods love a bit of salt. Sour lime with salt and tequila is lip-smackingly intense, and Japanese cookery is the master of sour and salty converging for inspired food moments.

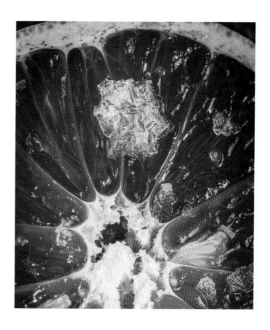

Sweet and Salty

Sweetness indicates a food that's high in energy and we crave it in a similar way to salt. When available, we are programmed to desire both. This hidden urge can tempt us with greed and over-seasoning, or consuming more sugar than we really need. I constantly remind myself to try to want less from my food and accept more of its raw flavour. This may seem contrary to the role of a chef but, in order to taste the inherent balance of an ingredient and enhance those levels, I try to only add what is needed, rather than always trying to change food for the sake of it. Cooking like this takes great self-control and sometimes I confess I drive full-speed into hedonism and excess. This is where sweet and salty steal my cooking soul away from the sensible. The two tastes collide to explode on the palate like fireworks. Like a moth to the flame, sweet and salty are entrancing. I've written a whole section of recipes on sweet and salty, simmering with mischief like a kitchen trickster at work.

Umami

Umami is a taste full of proteins and complex savoury notes that burst the speakers when you add salt. Some of the most iconic umami-rich ingredients and flavours are cemented into our seasoned larder culture. Imagine a world without Worcestershire sauce, anchovies, miso, bacon, seaweed or soy sauce. This umami-studded cast are glistening with natural salt. If you want to cook with gusto, then use salt alongside umami for an action-packed double act.

Intensity

The intensity of seasoning comes as the concentration of salt is increased and salinity goes up and so the flavours become more and more intense. This saltiness is perceived as pleasant – up to a certain point. We are aiming for the optimal level of salt or bliss point at the top of the curve, where salt added reaches maximum pleasure. This bliss point shifts from one person to another and there is no exact point, but instead a range to aim for that works when seasoning food. Therefore, when you are gradually increasing the seasoning as you cook a meal, adding salt in layers, pinch by pinch and tasting along the way, you have a better chance of reaching the sweet spot.

Remember to keep tasting and you should notice the palpable difference, the curve of pleasure that each flake of salt adds. Build intensity – don't just try to do it all in a moment.

(Opposite)
Top, right: Chicken salad with bitter leaves, hummus, zoug and roasted grapes.
Bottom, right: One of my favourite sweet and salty combinations is peach, mascarpone, thyme and toasted seeds with sea salt flakes to season.

Chapter Six
My Salt Sommelier Guide

I am a self-confessed salt geek. I encourage you to break cover and raise your head if someone seasons your food with dreadful abandon or, if it's bland, asks for some salt. Why not even take your own salt with you in a pinch pot discreetly hidden in your bag.

My job as a chef is to choose and pair the right salts to particular foods. Most of the time, any salt will do the job of enhancing flavour. But if you have some time, you can think about the finer things. Should I finish this venison carpaccio with a flick of smoked sea salt crystals for a woody, bonfire hit? What about a pinch of light powdered shio flakes over this grilled watermelon and burrata salad? My point is to make time to finish food properly. We make space for chilling a crisp white wine before serving, but do we think about what salt to use on a fillet steak?

As a general rule, firstly learn when to use salts for certain occasions. Some salt lends itself to the early stages of cooking to fortify the cooking process and strengthen the inherent flavours of the food. Salts that I reach for early on when cooking include a fine flake that dissolves quickly in water for boiling vegetables in a hurry, or a crunchy *sel gris* or coarse rock crystal salt for cooking meats on a hot seasoned griddle. The coarser salts provide a salty trivet to allow heat to sear but not char meats with a harsh crust and thus allow them longer in the pan without drying out too quickly. Textured salts are also excellent for making rustic salt doughs for baking – like wet gravel sand on the tideline, salt doughs trap in moisture like a seawall built with a bucket and spade. Other salts are the salts that you want to serve at the table or what I call a finishing salt – these tend to be flavoured salts I've made or show-stopping beautiful flakes full of flavour and ornate structure.

I will suggest some classic partnerships over the course of this book, but, like wine, ultimately, it's your choice and there is no one rule that applies to every meal. Have fun and enjoy discovering your own winning salt-pairing combinations!

(Opposite) Salts are good to store in a sealed family tiffin box for seasoning to suit every recipe. Treat them like spices, each with a unique flavour profile that can radically change a dish.
(Right) Beet salt

Be creative and use salt to finish your food with a flourish. Never be apologetic about seasoning and always serve salt as an option at the table. I do let people know as I'm serving if I have fully seasoned a dish or whether they may like to taste it and season to their personal preference. More often than not, I prefer to season at the last minute and then leave room for a finishing salt at the table where my friends and family can get interactive with their food and encourage them to taste, assess and adapt to appreciate the food.

If I could, I would season every plate of food bespoke for their personal taste, but I also love the way it passes the torch to them and it's my way of saying my job here is done. Over to you now to tailor the plate to your taste.

Merroir

The word 'terroir' is used to describe how the soil, microclimate and production methods impact on the flavour of wines. I think that the seawater and mineral composition used in salt makes as much if not more of an impact on taste. *Merroir* is a

word that is often used for oyster tasting and it's perfect for a salt sommelier. The mineral geology of a stretch of shoreline where sea salt is made, the level of salinity in a certain patch of sea, and the seasonal climate all make a huge difference (notwithstanding the artisan processes and rate of crystallisation in the evaporation tanks that also have an impact on the end taste profile). Some salts will have briny flavours perfect for seafood that come from an intense sweet calcium flavour, while others with more bitter potassium are better with grilled meats or sweet caramelised onions.

The salinity of seawater in the Atlantic is different compared to the Mediterranean, so even when salts are made using similar methods, you will taste a pronounced difference when trying salts from around the world.

Talking About Salt

Try comparing the taste of different salts on thin slices of cucumber, spread some unsalted butter on bread and season it with a pinch of salt to appreciate the flavour, make a batch of popcorn and taste the difference that salt makes on the puffed kernels, or scatter a pinch of salt over some grapefruit segments. If you want to have some fun afterwards, play word association with the salts and tastes they conjured up for you. Explore a new vocabulary to describe what you taste. I always find myself returning to the coast and landscape of the sea for inspiration to best describe my tastes, but it'd be great to know what you detect and how you describe it. There are no rules with this, because taste is so subjective, you can't go wrong.

For example, when I taste Cornish salt, I get a fractured salt, irregular and broken with good body

(Right) Salt and pepper

that crunches between my teeth. It dissolves in waves of briny sweet gorse nectar with a sharp sea breeze stinging the tongue. A calcium mineral tang, with clean sea foam sweeping sweet, umami crystals across my mouth in ripples. It isn't acrid, bitter or sulphuric. I don't find it delicate or fine, and these observations start to tell me that I could use it in a chocolate brownie to provide a salty crunch, or liberally sprinkled on bold seafood dishes with lots of lemon, and it's just about subtle enough to throw in a floral flavoured blend with rose and pink peppercorn. I wouldn't jump to using it on a dirty steak because it is on the lighter spectrum of salts in terms of depth of seasoning, but for me, it would perfectly suit a roast chicken with thyme as it leaves a sweet note on the tongue.

My point is, take a few moments when a pan of water is coming to the boil and taste what you've got in your kitchen before jumping to conclusions about how to use it. Good cooks prioritise time getting to know their ingredients and suppliers. Demystify salt first and it'll empower you to serve tastier food. Plus you can share what you know with friends and help build the new salt language.

Salt and Pepper

A classic culinary duo that are almost always talked about in the same breath. But next time you reach for the pepper – ask does pepper really belong in the recipe? Avoid robotic routine with food and instead consider your ingredients first. Remember that salt is one of five tastes and pepper is just one of hundreds of spices. For example, if you are cooking a Middle Eastern-inspired dish, go for some za'atar with your salt. The French and Italians love salt and pepper so it's abundant in their recipes, but in Scandinavia, you will often find sugar, pine or dried berries paired with salt, while Indian cuisine loves to use cumin seeds or chilli powder with salt.

Chapter Seven
My Favourite Salts

I have an extensive collection of salts that I enjoy cooking with in my kitchen. There are some that I buy again and again, and I feel this mix of salts provides me with a versatile palette to cook with. Like an artist painting with a set of familiar colours but with infinite scope to blend, a chef aims to brighten the eyes as much as enlivening taste buds. There is a multiverse of cubes, flakes, hoppers, pyramids and fused shards to choose from. Some have an immense surface area made of crannies and crevices laminated and encrusted with a mineral-rich glaze from the bittern. Other salts are milled for convenience or are brightly coloured to shock and awe.

All my favourites are excellent culinary salts, but there are just as many that I've not included which are special in different ways. Like learning about wine, there are many factors that make a difference to the end flavour – process, minerals and the *merroir*. The tastes are unique in their own way, but never forget that salt needs to be paired with food to really come alive and it's the way that different salts respond to food which creates a gallery of flavours.

African Pearl

An unusually-shaped sea salt that resembles small pea-sized pellets. It is found on the edge of the Namib desert and is made from the unusual combination of Atlantic winds and seawater rolling onto the southwestern African coastline. The movement in the salt pans from the warm swell curves the salt as it falls into the evaporating brine. It has low moisture so is also good for a grinder or mill. I find it has an intense clean, almost sweet flavour.

(Left) Rock salt   *(Below) African pearl*

Bamboo Salt

Containing bamboo leaf extracts, bamboo salt has been prized in China for its health properties for thousands of years. The colour pops on salads, seafood and with fruit salad.

Black Truffle Salt

The ultimate luxury salt that is blended with white sea salt flakes and speckled with black truffle. It normally has a low moisture content to keep the dried truffle preserved. Superb for finishing scrambled eggs or adding depth to mushrooms. Tastes woody, a bit like dried fruit leather with a deep earthy flavour.

Bolivian Rose

This striking rock salt has a soft, clementine colour mixed with a salmon pink hue. I think it looks like edible rose quartz gravel and is the closest you will get to eating semi-precious gemstones. Beautiful in a salt grinder and very tasty for cooking or finishing. Mild mineral sweet finish on the tongue.

Cornish Sea Salt

My local sea salt has a zesty, mineral tang. In texture, it has moderate moisture and a subtle bittersweet metallic note. The bright and oceanic taste makes it excellent with seafood. I've been using this salt for a very long time and think it's a great workhorse for cooking at home with artisan quality while also being of a good consistent quality.

(Opposite, clockwise from top left) Bamboo salt, Bolivian rose, black truffle salt

Cyprus Black

Among the most impressive sea salts I've ever used, these diamond-shaped massive pyramids range from intense jet black to charcoal-grey in colour, with very little to no moisture. This makes them ideal for finishing and they possess a tannic crunchy quality. Bold and subtle at the same time – an oxymoron perfect for finishing a dish with contrast and leaving a question hanging.

Fiore di Sale

The Italian version of *fleur de sel*. This salt is silver-white, angular and fine. I find it has a soft sodium profile, and the magnesium and potassium that adorn the flakes make it well rounded. Made on the Sicilian coast in solar evaporated salt pans since 800 BC.

Fleur de sel de Guérande

A wondrous handmade sea salt that is geographically protected with an *appellation d'origine contrôlée* in order to support the local economy and help preserve traditional production methods. The silver-white, fine irregular flakes have a moderate moisture and complex briny taste imparted by minerally clay. The *fleur de sel* from Ile de Ré is rose-tinged and well balanced with a mineral tang and subtle bitterness. Both are normally found as fine flakes. A multi-functional salt, but I normally reserve it for finishing.

Himalayan Pink

Also known as Pakistani *namak*, this mined rock salt is coloured pink by the iron oxide or rust in the salt. The blood red to peach pink colours can be extremely attractive and the flavour has a gentle metallic profile. Widely available as salt blocks or as bowls for cooking with. Himalayan Pink salt is not the same as the pink salt used for curing that contains nitrates and/or nitrites. Commercial curing salts such as Prague Powder #1 and #2 are coloured so that they are not consumed raw by mistake and are functional salts for curing rather than seasoning.

(Opposite, top) Cyprus black
(Opposite, bottom left) Fleur de sel
(Opposite left and above) Himalayan Pink

Kala Namak

This rock salt from Pakistan is a real powerhouse. The purplish-brown gravel texture doesn't promise much, but it has a strong sulphuric, pine sweetness. Good with browned meats, game and roasted root vegetables. Use as a finishing salt or to boost umami profiles in mushroom recipes.

Maldon Salt

Synonymous with British flaked sea salt. This white Essex salt is reliable, clean, bright and crisp. For me, it lacks the same mineral complexity of some sea salts, but it always looks and feels fantastic to use. The hollow pyramid flakes make an excellent finishing salt as they dissolve quickly on the tongue after a light crunch.

Murray River Salt Flakes

Tiny pinkish Australian flakes with a fruity bark flavour and apricot hue. Carotene is secreted from salt-tolerant algae in the brine which gives the salt its peachy colour. High in calcium, so it's extra sweet tasting, it's perfect for barbecued meats and shellfish, plus it's low in moisture, meaning it can be finely milled for an even coverage.

Persian Blue

A very rare Iranian rock salt, it is taken from a single seam running through ancient salt beds. It comes as an irregular gravel texture or as larger rock salt crystals with no moisture. Cool, mild mineral sweet taste.

Red Alaea

This brick-red Hawaiian sea salt has a long mineral finish. The red clay in the natural salt pans where it is produced makes it brightly coloured with a sweet jerky tang and it pairs well with Spanish and Cajun flavours. I recommend using it for barbecue cures or as a finishing salt. The gravel texture is also available more finely milled. Grind it in a pestle and mortar to soften the texture and for finer seasonings.

(Opposite, clockwise from top left)
Kala namak, Red Alaea, Persian blue

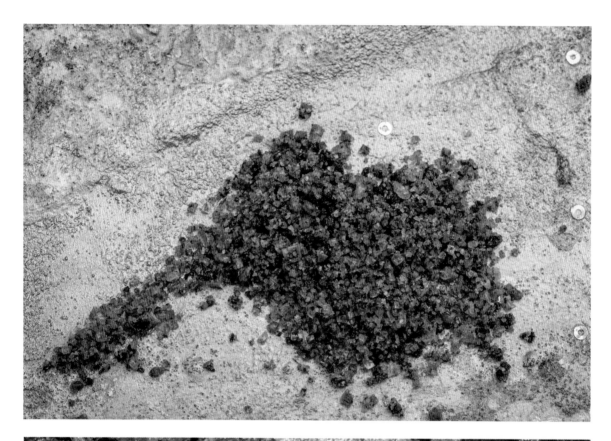

Sal de Gusano

I love this traditional blended salt, but some people find it a bit much. Made from the worms taken off agave plants that are sun-dried or oven-roasted and mixed with chilli and sea salt for an earthy fiery flavour, in Mexico, this is used to pair with mezcal. Smoky, roasted taste like cumin, but with a hint of sweetness. Can be mild to very spicy.

Sel Gris

This grey sea salt is another French classic. Small to medium grains, minerally intense, faint clay back notes, sweet and grassy with a robust metallic finish. Superb for cooking with in the earlier stages of a recipe as it is affordable to buy in bulk and robust tasting for building layers of flavour early in the cooking process. Think of *sel gris* as a bit like laying bricks with mortar – it fortifies food and sets strong foundations, but is unlikely to be used as a seasoning for finishing as it can taste a little coarse and harsh.

Smoked Salt

Any type of salt can be smoked, but it is often done with extravagant-looking flakes or crystals and used as a finishing salt. The salt itself is slow smoked normally over hard woods like oak, cherry, apple and hickory. It takes a long time to produce but provides a superb seasoning. I also smoke finer flakes and milled rock salts to use in barbecue rubs and cures. Smoked salt delivers a caramel sweet layer of woody flavour to a dish. It's a must have salt for any seasoned cook to keep close at hand in the kitchen.

Storing Salts

Keep open salts that you use regularly in the kitchen near to the stove. Store in salt boxes or cellars – something that is large enough to get your hand into easily. I also like open salt pigs which are normally ceramic.

I have a collection of pinch pots at the table to finish food (and to show off!), functional pots of salt for cooking, large wide bowls with lids for catering, and a huge collection of world salts and homemade seasonal salts in my studio that I then store in dark, sealed containers – I keep colourful flavoured salts made with fresh ingredients away from direct sunlight to avoid discolouration.

Store all salt sealed to keep out moisture where possible. There is no shelf life on salt apart from salts flavoured with organic materials, which I use within 2–3 months.

(Opposite, top) Worm salt
(Left) Chicken salt – A great flavoured salt to capture the essence of a roast chicken dinner (see page 197).
(Right) Mint salt – Nothing smells fresher than a bowl of mint salt (see page 206). The colour adds a pop of bright green to any summer dish, and it works well when seasoning a cucumber yogurt or courgette salad.

Chapter Eight
Measuring Salt

I used my Instagram channel the other day to ask for some advice on how best to describe a pinch of salt. The answers that came back were great and it was really interesting to see how much nostalgia is mixed in with our notions of salt with old-fashioned words and memories from older generations.

I think we've become a little detached from measuring salt and I want to help you correct this balance by encouraging you to find your pinch again. Collectively, we've forgotten how to season and I think it is an essential lost skill to relearn with a flash, a flicker or a faint spark to illuminate your food again.

What is a Pinch?

A pinch of salt to me is the single most powerful kitchen tool. I taught my children (although we always call it a pipkin at home) how to season with a pinch of salt incredibly early, when they were starting to beat eggs, chop vegetables and keep the kitchen tidy.

Determining, for example, what one level teaspoon of salt is won't be identical every time as one salt is not the same as another. The crystalline shape and structure vary enormously from one salt to another, so the volume of space they occupy can be very different and, to be fair, even one spoon can be very different to another spoon, so finding accurate measurements of seasoning within recipes is tricky. This constant desire for standardised food is part of a heavily processed food culture that's lost the beauty of independent artisan craft.

A pinch of salt is the ultimate artisan measurement, almost impossible to define and standardise as a weight or volume. This makes it ethereal and elusive, unique and special. The amount of salt you add in a pinch carefully balances the scales of a dish, wavering on the fulcrum – success or lacklustre blandness on a knife-edge. No pressure then! Learning how to salt to taste is an opportunity to take an everyday act and redefine it as mastering salt craft. This may sound grand, but I recommend that you practise until you know the power between your fingers.

For me, measuring salt is instinctive rather than precise and I honestly believe that's the best way to work with ingredients. On their own terms rather than with a strict system we've created with one rule for everything. Cook and season by taste for best results. That is what I'd like as an epitaph on all my recipes. Make them your own and build your confidence to take the reins of your salt. You tell me what a pinch is! Frankly, yours will be different to mine and that's what I love about food.

Salt Mindfully

I'm obstinately against mindfulness as a trendy label and lifestyle choice. It all feels a bit of a fad to me which gets caught up in sharing that mindfulness as a preachy status update rather than the real deal. That said, I love the notion of finding peace in the moment with simple focus and how often quiet repetition leads to joy. For me, salting is a mindful activity. Handling salt is therapeutic and tactile, both an act of concentration yet also of letting go. The nerves in my fingertips are massaged by tiny crystals and flakes, and the touch awakens my senses.

Cooking is rarely identical when repeated and replicated. As a food writer, I know that despite my best endeavours, people rarely use the same pot with the exact same chicken and similar-sized dice of vegetables every time. So, my best advice is to rely on your tongue as a tool to achieve some consistency. Taste every time you cook until you learn how your pinches of salt work for your palate when cooking at home.

Strategic Ingredient

Handle salt regularly and remember that how and when you tactically use it in a dish is the best way to elevate your food. But before you learn how to season, you need a strategy.

It's essential to adapt the way you cook to focus on each salt's own minerals, moisture level and taste. If you have a very dry salt, it will stick better to something like popcorn compared to a moist salt.

Using a sweet salt in a salted caramel means you can use less sugar when balancing the flavour. Plan to use a salt early in the process to start osmosis or diffusion ahead of cooking. Curing can be such a helpful tool once you understand the power of pre-salting before you cook food – osmosis and diffusion can draw out moisture if you want to dry something or make food juicier. Much depends on how and when you use salt in a recipe, not just how much. A fine flake will dissolve more quickly than traditional crystals, so you can add it later in the cooking process.

As a very general rule, I use 1 per cent salt for meats, fish and vegetables and then increase to 2 per cent for blanching water. The amount of salt you add makes a huge difference, so study quantities as best you can, but also take any instruction with a pinch of salt and remember to fall back on your own tasting instinct – does it taste good to you?

The Act of Salting

Before I tell you all my tricks, let me reiterate one more time that inexactness is okay. Pay close attention to the character of your ingredients and the salts you are using. Adjust the seasoning according to how the flavours are developing. It is only at the end of cooking, as you sit down to eat, that it should be in perfect harmony – and even then, you can add a pinch of salt at the table to finish it off. It's so much easier to add salt than it is to try and take it out, so err on the side of caution. Be diligent, delicate, bold and patient when salting.

The Pinch

My pinch is not for large items of food but rather single ingredients – a dressing, to finish a dish or for a slight alteration in flavour. A pinch is excellent to deliver the detail. Try to work with precision and consider each bite.

Take some flakes or fine rock salt between your forefinger and thumb. I then gently rub to release the salt and sometimes to grind a large flake into finer shards for better coverage.

Season from above but not too high up. You want

to control the fall with delicate accuracy. A good pinch of salt encourages thought and consideration of why you are seasoning, where and when.

Double up with two pinches when you take a large pinch of salt between your thumb, forefinger and middle finger – this is sometimes referred to as a dash, a taste or a hint. Half a pinch is a smidgen.

To sprinkle with salt, for me, normally means to take a large pinch or dash of salt and raise your hand a little higher. Moving your hand from side to side while rubbing the salt between your fingers is a great way to sprinkle a dish with salt for a light seasoning.

If I want to get a more intense sprinkle or even covering for something like a large belly pork or side of salmon, then I may choose to sprinkle with a wrist shake for more salt.

The Flick

This motion is often overlooked but has a useful place in seasoned salt craft. Flicking salt is superb for seasoning when you are cooking over flames or a hot grill. When working a busy set of pans, it is also quick, fast and extends the range you can effectively season from.

Flicking salt takes a little more practise and can be messy – so I tend to use it more when cooking outdoors. Sometimes, when you have seasoned something with a pinch, you will notice flakes and salt crystals clinging to your fingers. The flick is an excellent way to use those last bursts of salt accurately, for micro seasoning a part of a plate with a touch more salt. Like percussion punctuating an orchestra, the flick of salt is a triangle or a tambourine adding the lightest extra note, but it can make all the difference when composing something special.

The Two-finger Grind

A supremely satisfying large pinch or dash of salt that enables you to really work a flake or crystal down into finer parts. You could use a pestle and mortar to grind salt at home, but I love this salt rubbing motion to mill down larger flakes into less ostentatious functional seasoning for a dish.

(*Top*) *Flick*
(*Right*) *Two-finger grind*

Wrist Shake

I learned this motion when I was running my old pastry company, when I used to flour the marble blocks with a light covering of flour before rolling out pastry.

The action is a bit like shaking dice if you were playing snake eyes in Vegas. In fact, always have a closed palm practice to find the motion and then let the salt go through the gaps in your fingers and out of the top of your loose fist each time you shake your wrist. It's a heavily directional way of seasoning that tends to skim across sideways, so turn the food around to cover evenly on both sides of the surface. Great when using large amounts of salt or if you want to spread it out across the surface of a large roasting tin quickly.

The Palmful

I only use a palmful of salt for large pots or cooking water and wet cures. It's an easy way of grabbing a handful of salt to throw into a pan and a useful way of getting all the salt in with one movement.

It's something I tend to use with coarse, thicker-grained salts like *sel gris* or traditional crystals and when making dry cures or salt baking. These salts run through your palm well and can be added in a large handful to a stockpot or when mixing a dough for salt baking.

The Salt Shower

This upright motion is the most Zen of my salting methods. All four fingers and thumb face downwards and, holding a big handful of salt, you move the fingers and thumb up and down loosely together, alternating like grinding pistons. This movement showers salt down slowly and with a bit of lateral movement thrown in, like a claw circulating over a barrel of soft fairground prizes below.

You can easily add more salt to large cuts of meat, whole root vegetables or fish. This is smooth, gravity fed, simple and helpful for getting a large amount of salting done with good control but very little effort.

(Opposite, clockwise from top left)
Wrist wag, palmful, salt falls

Other Ways to Season

Finishing Flakes

This hardly counts as a way to measure salt, but it is impressive to master when plating up. Placing salt carefully to finish a dish individually can look fantastic and guarantees great placement for crunch or visual contrast. Clean, pyramidal salt flakes, ice white pearls or crunchy crystals look mesmerising, so I sometimes, though very rarely, use chef's tweezers here.

Grinding Rock Salt

For super fine seasoning with rock salt, get yourself a salt grater or try using a nutmeg grater. This is a lovely tool to season dishes at the table and adds a little theatre. And because rock salt has very low moisture, it's a good salt to add to things like popcorn or fried chicken.

Micro Seasoning

Season in layers for best results. Taste and adjust again and again. As you add ingredients, process or transform them, this is when you need to amp up the flavour. Seasoning food from within at every stage of cookery.

Embodied Salt

Salt also occurs naturally in many foods and offers a fantastic secondary layer of seasoning when cooking. Seaweed, soy sauce, miso, capers and anchovies are my favourite ingredients for a naturally salty inclusion in a dish which provide a delicate way to add saltiness and umami depth of flavour without reaching for a pinch of salt.

Seasoning Water

Probably the first stage when micro seasoning is to use salted water for vegetables or pasta. You just want the salinity to provide the memory of the sea if you taste it rather than the actual 3.5 per cent that tastes unpalatable and costs more every time in the amount of salt you use. Pasta dough is not usually seasoned much or at all so Italians season their water heavily as a way to balance the dish. Seasoning water is a perfect example of micro seasoning in action and makes a big difference.

Don't forget that you will throw most of the water away, but the salt is essential for seasoning pasta as well as for the processes of diffusion, brining and wet curing to be effective. Put your salt in the water early so that it dissolves into a solution before you cook. Essentially aim to cook everything in brine for food with radical levels of flavour. This way you may not need to add much, if any, salt, when you serve food. The crunch, texture and pop of salt onto already perfectly seasoned vegetables finishes a dish off but shouldn't be how we season in isolation.

The Salt Spectrum

People season differently all over the world. The French, broadly speaking, season their *pain au levain* (so it tastes amazing) with unsalted butter. Tuscan bread isn't seasoned much, but everything else is heavily seasoned. In Japan, steamed rice is unseasoned but is surrounded by very tasty salty sauces and fermented flavours.

There is no universal rule on how much to salt. If food tastes flat, you can normally point the finger at under-seasoning. When you are cooking, take a small spoonful and taste test everything, then season a second spoonful with a small pinch of salt before seasoning the whole meal.

Put this book down now and go and get a mug or utensil holder and place some spoons in it. Keep that little spoon caddy right there, next to your stove and taste everything you cook. One of the greatest kitchen tools I can share is to season to taste.

Salt Geek

What do you do if you have over-salted your food?

Either admit defeat, throw it away and start again, or you can try to dilute the food to reduce the salinity. Halving the amount of your dish and bulking it up with more ingredients can be a quick rescue. I will also use lemon juice or vinegar if I've over-seasoned – yes, even a seasoned chef occasionally adds a pinch too much salt!

Alternatively, you can transform the dish completely, for example, by taking a salty vegetable purée and re-imagining it as a soup by adding lots more stock, or shredding the salty duck and mixing it with a plum sauce and charred spring onions. Large chunks of raw potato can be added to an overly salted dish like soup to absorb some of the salt and can then be removed before serving. That said, the most effective way to solve the problem is to add salt gradually – it's much harder to remove salt from food than it is seasoning in stages.

Try to avoid food waste, but if something tastes too salty, don't eat it. Our taste buds have evolved to serve as much as a warning mechanism as they are as pleasure-givers.

My Salt Craft

Part Three

Chapter Nine
Dry Curing

Probably the simplest salt craft skill of all is to dry cure food, where ingredients are coated in a layer of salt to draw out moisture and intensify their flavour over time. Salt-based cures not only preserve food but also change their texture and make them uninhabitable for unwanted bacteria and mould, while a quick cure before cooking will make all the difference to your recipe. Here are mineral-crusted meats and fish to tantalise your taste buds and tickle your fancy.

How it Works

Salt-preservation techniques may have changed over the years, but the science behind them remains the same and is as useful today as it was a thousand years ago.

The basic principle of a dry cure is to rub salt into the surface of your food and then the salt crystals kill the *Clostridium botulinum* bacteria. These dry cures stop food from going off by drawing out the moisture of food-spoiling bacteria and, as these unwanted bacteria decrease, other beneficial bacteria such as *Lactobacillus* can flourish.

As salt is left in contact with food, its chemical properties trigger a unique reaction in raw food, enhancing flavours and drawing out moisture via osmosis to suppress the growth of bacteria and so collapsing their cells. Osmosis is a process that takes

place across the surface of the food where moisture is slowly drawn out, then some of the dissolved salts penetrate back into the cells of the food, seasoning it while it cures. This is what gives many cured foods their distinctive sour tangy flavour. Smoking and air drying are also used as extra steps in tandem with dry curing to boost the preservation process and add more depth of flavour.

For curing, I always use a good sea salt with high levels of magnesium, as this mineral helps to firm up proteins and gives the finished food a pleasantly firm texture.

Salting Pre-cooking

I use cures all the time as part of my pre-cooking ritual to prepare food for the pan. These are quick cures, often taking only a few minutes, sometimes

> **Top Tip**
>
> *Wild garlic flowers also provide delicious capers after blooming. Dry cure the capers packed in salt in a jar and allow a brine to form. Keep sealed for 2–3 months and refrigerate once you start using them. Delicious in pasta sauces.*

(Left) Line-caught Cornish mackerel, ready to be filleted and cured.

several hours. Curing to me is a foundation for good cooking.

The process improves the produce you use, so that your work is already on the right path before you introduce any heat. For example, a lightly cured fillet of cod will respond far better when fried in butter than using wet fish straight from the market. Even 30–40 minutes of light curing can make a huge difference – especially with seafood. Joints of meat should, as a matter of routine, be salted the day before cooking and left in the fridge overnight for better results.

You can make a quick cure mix with herbs and spices, but for speed, pre-salting or quick cures can be 100 per cent sea salt. Lightly season the food for an even coverage and leave on a wire rack in the fridge so air can circulate around it. Put the rack on a drip tray with a sheet of kitchen paper to absorb any water that's drawn out. You can rinse off and pat dry the meat or fish before cooking, but I find this counter-intuitive as you are re-introducing water before cooking. If you have cured your produce before cooking, remember that you may not require as much salt when cooking at later stages.

Lightly curing with salt prior to cooking is a great way to develop flavour and improve the texture of food, but it won't preserve your food.

The Basics

Longer cures require time to work their magic. Cure ratios will differ widely depending on what you are curing, but the mix of salt I use is generally 3:1 salt to sugar. Use approximately 100g/3½oz of cure mix per 1kg/2lb 4oz of meat or fish.

Make more cure mix than you need for the first salting and store in a labelled, sealed container. This way you can top up your cures every couple of days over the course of a week. Refreshing the cure allows the balance of flavour to develop consistently across the surface as opposed to changing the salt and hydration levels in localised parts, as a brine forms on certain patches of the meat.

I always use a similar set of curing spices and will sometimes introduce vinegar or a flavoursome spirit to give them a little more zing. The core spices I normally associate with curing are: cloves, black peppercorns, fennel seeds, coriander seeds, mustard seeds and chilli. Others that often make regular appearances include dried juniper berries, star anise, allspice and cinnamon. Citrus works very well in cures, so always consider adding some grated orange, lemon or lime zest. Finally, robust herbs such as bay, sage, rosemary and thyme also work well – avoid wet, oily herbs like basil, coriander and parsley.

Sweet Cures

I sometimes refer to these as soft cures. The idea is to use a ratio of 2:1 salt to sugar so that the harsh saltiness is reduced. However, in my personal

(Above) Hot-smoked duck that has been cured using smoked sea salt, served with pickled cabbage, toasted walnuts and quince.

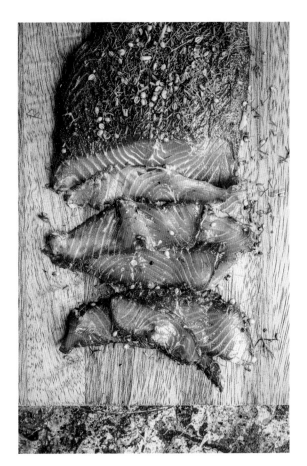

(Above) Gravlax cured with coriander seeds, dill and grated red cabbage for a gorgeous purple colour and cruciferous earthy flavour.

You don't need any professional kit to dry cure at home. That said, ceramic, plastic or non-reactive metal are the best containers to cure in. Stainless steel is okay, but can rust after prolonged use, so I recommend ceramic or plastic.

Cheesecloth or muslin helps hugely when curing for longer lengths of time to keep flies off the surface while allowing airflow, and mesh racking can be helpful to prevent dry-cured foods from sitting in their own brine. Large food containers make it easier to dry cure hams and large joints of meat in the fridge. Get yourself some butcher's string and hooks for air drying once curing is complete.

experience, this also makes them less effective for long-term curing as the sugar can invite bacterial growth and facilitate fermentation, so I use this with fish for 24–48 hour cures or smaller items of meat like duck breasts that I intend to hot smoke.

I'm very influenced by Nordic cures that balance sugar and salt with herbs and aromatics so well – try adding dill, juniper or seaweed. Most of the time, I suggest using light soft brown sugar for sweet cures, but for a twist, you can use a combination of molasses, black treacle or dark soft brown sugar. Honey and salt also make a delicious dry cure for garlic cloves.

(Above) My dry-curing blend with aromatic spices and plenty of citrus zest. Perfect for confited duck or curing mackerel.

How to Dry Cure Belly Pork

Bacon takes time and planning – dry-curing pork belly in sea salt and brown sugar takes at least 1 week – so as you gain confidence, try to work ahead of yourself, with cuts at different stages of curing. There's nothing more satisfying than finishing a slab of home-cured bacon and not having to wait another few weeks before your next rasher. Dry curing in succession is a good way to always have something delicious in the fridge.

Serves 4

1–2kg/2lb 4oz–4lb 8oz boneless
   belly pork

For the cure
600g/1lb 5oz sea salt crystals
200g/7oz light soft brown sugar
1 tsp dried juniper berries
1 tsp fennel seeds
1 tsp dried chilli flakes
1 tsp yellow mustard seeds
1 tsp black peppercorns
1 tsp coriander seeds
600ml/1 pint stout (optional)
2 tbsp black treacle (optional)

Pat the belly pork dry with a sheet of kitchen paper. In a large mixing bowl, mix together all the cure ingredients except for the stout and treacle (if using). If you want to try using these, do so after the first 4 days of curing by adding them to the remaining cure and then rubbing into the pork belly that is curing.

Rub 200g/7oz of the cure all over the pork and keep the rest in a sealed jar in a cupboard. Place the pork in a suitable covered container in the fridge.

After 2 days, replace the cure by rubbing it off the pork with a sheet of kitchen paper or a stiff brush, then rubbing the pork with another fresh 200g/7oz of the cure, cover and return to the fridge. Repeat every couple of days, pouring away any brine that collects. After 1 week, brush off the cure and wrap the bacon in cheesecloth or muslin. Tie the cheesecloth/muslin around the bacon and hang it up somewhere cool and well ventilated to air dry, or hang in the fridge.

You can then cold-smoke the bacon or cook it. You should notice far less water coming out of the sliced bacon if you cook it in a pan and a wonderful mildly spiced aroma as it fries. Dry-cured bacon also crisps up better when cooked, so if you love a caramelised rasher of umami-packed pork, then you'll love this salted bacon!

Keep the bacon refrigerated in an airtight container and use within 2 weeks.

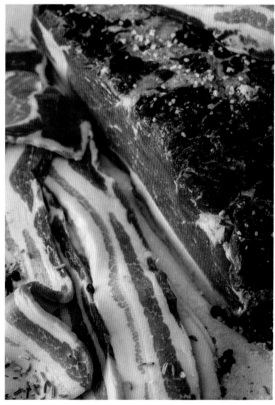

How to Make Beef Jerky

This recipe is an absolute knockout. I took my love of dried meat and freshly ground coffee and threw them together. The key to success with beef jerky is remembering to rinse off the cure thoroughly after it's been allowed to do its job. I have repeatedly tried leaving some of the spiced crystals on the beef while it dries, only to regret it later when it tastes too salty. The cure will build mountains of flavour into the beef and draw out moisture before it hits the dehydrator, but it does not need any extra salt left on the surface.

Serves 6

½ tsp dried wild thyme

1 tsp smoked garlic powder

1 tsp coriander seeds

1 tsp smoked dried chilli flakes

1 tsp smoked paprika

½ tsp ground white pepper

3 tbsp sea salt

1 tbsp light soft brown sugar

1 tbsp coffee beans

225g/8oz sirloin steak, fat trimmed off
  and thinly sliced

To make the cure, grind the thyme, garlic powder, all the spices, the salt, sugar and coffee beans together in a large pestle and mortar or spice grinder.

Toss the sliced beef in the cure to evenly coat and leave covered in a glass bowl or tray in the fridge for 2 days.

Wash under cold running water to remove the cure, then pat dry. Place in a dehydrator or a preheated (fan-assisted, if possible) oven at 70°C fan/160°F/gas mark as low as you can go, for 6–8 hours.

Once dried and cooled, store in an airtight container in a cool, dry place and consume within 3–4 weeks.

How to Make Gravlax

In your curing repertoire, mastering a good gravlax is essential. I love playing with aromatic herbs in my fish cure, a splash of unusual botanical spirit, bold spices and grated vegetables. Red cabbage can provide a lovely purple dye, grated turmeric root for yellow and spice, charcoal or soy sauce for striking black colours. Be adventurous and experiment with colour and flavour, but remember that there are certain recipes that stand the test of time for a reason. To me, the blend of earthy beetroot, anise from dill and bittersweet juniper gin goes beyond fashion and reveals true foodie style.

Serves 6

For the gravlax

1 large fillet of wild salmon

1 beetroot (about 115g/4oz), peeled
  and grated

4 tbsp dry gin

2 tbsp finely chopped dill

For the curing salt

4 tbsp Arctic sea salt

2 tbsp light soft brown sugar

2 tsp crushed dried juniper berries

2 tsp crushed coriander seeds

1 tsp cracked black pepper

Grated zest of 1 orange

½ tsp dried chilli flakes

½ tsp caraway seeds

Make the cure by mixing all the curing salt ingredients together in a large bowl. Transfer to a sealed container until you are ready to use it.

Remove the skin from the salmon and then rub in the curing salt, grated beetroot and gin all over the fish. Cover the salmon with any remaining cure that has not adhered to the fish so that it is evenly distributed on both sides of the fish, then place in a container in the fridge under a plate weighed down with rocks or some tins on top of it to help compress the cure.

Turn and re-weight/compress after 24 hours and cure for a total of 36–48 hours. The longer you leave it, the firmer the texture and more flavour you can work into the fish. Personally, I like a lighter cure, so tend to remove the fish from the cure and rinse after 36 hours.

Wash the salmon under cold running water to remove the excess cure. Pat dry and press the salmon into a tray of the finely chopped dill to coat.

Carve the salmon very thinly and serve with crackers, pickles or on blinis. It is also fantastic with scrambled eggs for brunch.

The gravlax will keep in an airtight container in the fridge for up to 2 weeks. It is best to keep it as a whole piece and carve it fresh as needed.

Salt Choice:

Arctic

I use an Icelandic salt for this gravlax cure as the flaky crystals are rich in magnesium, thus providing a sweet flavour to complement the beetroot. I also love the part that the Nordic landscape plays in its production, which gives this recipe a sense of story. Geothermal is the sole energy used for this form of Icelandic salt production, which takes hot geyser water from Reykjanes, rising at around 93°C/200°F, to preheat the brine and help with the drying process. A totally zero carbon and highly modern salt process with a history dating back two centuries. Sustainable methods producing a truly quality product – for me, it's the perfect salt for this wild salmon recipe.

Salt Cod

Salting cod is a method steeped in history that stretches across the Atlantic from the Arctic to Newfoundland and the coast of Portugal to the Caribbean. The discovery in the 1620s of rich cod stocks in cold Atlantic waters around Cape Cod led to huge trade expansion. The fishing ranged from the Portuguese mercantile navy, who fished in territories far from Porto across the Atlantic Ocean, to the Viking reliance on salted fish for their raiding and trading in the North.

The coast of Newfoundland and Massachusetts was peppered with salting houses in the early colonial era of North America and the production of salt cod in the Caribbean islands led to further extraction of spices and tobacco back to Europe. Salt cod has been hugely influential on the history of food and the wider movement of peoples. Where now people think of an army marching on its stomach, historically, a navy sailed on its salted stores.

Through osmosis, salt cod can lose 40–60 per cent of its water content as a result of the dry-curing process. This loss of moisture made it less heavy to ship and provided an impenetrable environment for bacteria, so it would not spoil on long voyages. Salt cod kept well, was relatively straightforward to cure on board or on the shore for a speedy transportation, and once desalted, it tasted great too which, compared to lots of preserved meat and fish of its time, must have been a pleasant bonus. Salt cod was a kind of Campbell's Soup success story of the eighteenth century and was one of the first mass-produced preserved foods.

The sustainable management of fish stocks today matters hugely to me as a chef living by the sea, and I find the continued growth of cod as one of Europe's and America's most popular fish extremely interesting as it demonstrates how clearly a single ingredient's history was predominantly shaped by salt. Before freezing became the norm, salting fish was the best way to move food over long distances. Nowadays, salt cod has lost its status as a commodity of trade but remains a firm favourite with food tourists and anthropologists alike. Personally, I love salt cod and really enjoy the thought of sharing this salt craft with you to try at home.

The basic dry-curing principle is one of the most satisfying ways to improve your seafood cookery and there's a reason that salted cod travelled the world and is still popular today. Salted fish retains flavour when cooked and can be firmer in the pan without flaking as quickly. Even a light cure for 30 minutes or so can improve a fillet before you cook it and lock in that fresh delicate fishy flavour.

How to Salt Cod

My salt cod recipe takes some preparation but is well worth the effort. I personally prefer the salting of my fish slightly on the lighter side when making it at home, especially if I am eating it that same week or within a day or two. On the other hand, if you are salting to preserve (or in the days before refrigeration), salt, time and patience are vital to successful curing.

Serves 2

2 MSC cod fillets, about 280g/10oz
  in total

2 tbsp Arctic sea salt flakes

To salt the cod, completely cover both fillets in a thinly sprinkled even coating of the sea salt flakes. Place them on a wire rack in the fridge for 5–7 days to allow airflow around the fish to help it dry as it cures. Place a sheet of kitchen paper on a tray under the fish to absorb water. Turn the fillets each day. You will notice the texture becoming increasingly firm to the touch.

After 5–7 days, wash off any remaining salt under cold running water, then soak the cod fillets in a bowl of water in the fridge for 12–24 hours. Refresh the water every 4–6 hours and discard the salty brine. You can do a quick taste test and cook a small piece of the fish to judge the salinity, then de-salt as before for a further 12–24 hours if you find the salinity still too pronounced.

Once the salt cod is to your taste, drain, then pat it dry and cook as required. If not using straight away, store it in an airtight container in the fridge for up to 5 days, before cooking.

Salt Choice:

Arctic

To salt my cod, I chose an Arctic salt that's been made using a geothermal method since 1753. The Nordur sea salt flakes have a sweet, crystal cold flavour with a clean and light texture. The tang reminds me of a citrus-rind-infused frozen vodka with a crunch like kindling on a still night. An enticing crackling bite under bright moonlight.

Salt Cod Kyiv

The garlic-herb butter filling and the breadcrumb crust on these Kyivs need no extra seasoning. The combination of crispy golden breadcrumbs with milky-white salted cod and an aromatic butter is comfort food on a plate. You can also try a variation on this recipe by making a curried butter filling instead for a Kyiv with a twist.

Serves 2

For the Kyivs
2 prepared Salt Cod fillets (soaked, drained and patted dry, see page 83), about 280g/10oz in total
1 tbsp plain flour
2 eggs, beaten
85g/3oz panko breadcrumbs
Vegetable oil, for frying

For the garlic-herb butter
85g/3oz unsalted butter, softened
2 garlic cloves, crushed
Grated zest of 1 lemon
1 tbsp finely chopped parsley

Make the garlic butter in advance by mixing the softened butter, garlic, lemon zest and parsley in a bowl with a fork. Form the flavoured butter into a cylinder and wrap in baking parchment. Freeze the butter until firm, so it's easy to portion later.

To prepare the Kyivs, insert a sharp knife into the thickest part of each salt cod fillet to make a tidy incision and create a cavity to stuff with the butter. Carefully push half of the frozen butter puck into the centre of each fillet. Dredge both fish fillets in plain flour, followed by beaten egg and finally cover in breadcrumbs. Repeat this process two or three times for a thick breadcrumb coating.

Pour enough oil into a frying pan to cover the base and heat it to 180°C/350°F, then cook the Kyivs for 4–5 minutes on each side until they reach an internal temperature of 65°C/150°F and the butter in the middle is melted and the breadcrumbs are golden all over.

Serve simply with some steamed vegetables on the side, dressed with a little lemon juice.

Salt Cod Beignets

This is my fun spicy Creole twist on a classic salt cod croquette. For this recipe, I use a blend of salt cod, spring onion, pepper and Cajun spices and deep-fry them like a New Orleans beignet. While they're still warm, try dusting in a hot pepper salt and serve with plenty of red-eye mayo on the side for dunking.

Serves 4

For the salt cod beignets
225g/8oz prepared Salt Cod fillets (soaked, drained and patted dry, see page 83) – cured using Atlantic salt (see Salt Choice opposite)

First, for the beignets, place the salt cod fillets in a small saucepan with the milk, onion and bay leaves. Poach the fish over a low heat for 5–10 minutes until it starts to flake apart easily. Strain the milk into a jug (discard the bay) and allow the fish, onion and milk to cool. Keep the milk to combine with the beignet batter later.

Cut the cod into small pieces. In a large mixing bowl, combine the flaked salt cod and onion with the red pepper, spring onion, flour,

225ml/8fl oz whole milk

½ onion, finely diced

1 bay leaf

½ red pepper, de-seeded and
   finely diced

1 spring onion, sliced

115g/4oz plain flour

1 tsp baking powder

1 tbsp hot pepper sauce

1 tbsp Cajun spice blend

Vegetable oil, for deep-frying

For the red-eye mayo

2 tbsp mayo

2 tsp espresso, at room temperature

1 tsp hot pepper sauce

1 tsp lemon juice (optional)

Sea salt and cracked black pepper

For the DIY hot pepper salt

2 tbsp sea salt flakes

1 tbsp light soft brown sugar

1 tsp smoked paprika

1 tsp dried thyme

1 tsp dried chipotle chilli flakes

½ tsp ground mace

baking powder, hot pepper sauce and Cajun spice blend. Gradually incorporate about 100ml/3½fl oz of the reserved milk. Stir constantly until you have a stiff batter similar in consistency to thick yogurt.

Allow the beignet batter to rest in the fridge while you make the red-eye mayo and hot pepper salt. For the red-eye mayo, simply whisk the mayo, espresso and hot pepper sauce together in a small bowl. Season to taste and try adding a little lemon juice to lift the acidity, if you like. Set aside.

To make the hot pepper salt, place all the ingredients in a food processor or spice grinder and blitz for a fine textured seasoning. Set aside.

To cook the beignets, pour enough vegetable oil into a large, deep, heavy-based saucepan so it comes about a third of the way up the sides (or use a deep-fat fryer) and heat over a medium heat until it reaches 180°C/350°F (or until a small piece of bread dropped in browns within 30 seconds). For each beignet, gently drop a heaped tablespoonful or ice-cream scoopful of the batter into the hot oil (cook the beignets in batches, a few at a time) and deep-fry for 3–4 minutes until they are golden brown and crispy on the outside. Using a slotted spoon, transfer the beignets to some kitchen paper to remove the excess oil, and keep warm. Repeat until all the beignets are cooked (bringing the oil back up to temperature before adding each batch).

Dust the hot pepper salt over the beignets or toss them gently in the spicy salt to season. Serve warm with the red-eye mayo on the side.

Salt Choice:

Atlantic

I chose an Atlantic salt from the coast of Portugal for the cod curing in this recipe. It has a tangy, almost sweet gorse flower flavour with large, pale, soft flakes that dissolve quickly on the surface of the fish for a smooth even cure.

How to Dry Cure Fish

Dry curing fish is a great routine to develop at home. The combination of curing with salt, sugar and spice gives fish a primed and ready-to-absorb rich, woody aroma when smoking. Consider the process as two-fold – on the one hand, dry curing fish preserves it by removing moisture and inhibiting bacterial growth, and on the other, it imparts flavour through osmosis and seasons the fish before smoking. As the salt and sugar dissolve on the fish and slowly move to areas of higher water concentration, they take the spices with them in the brine that forms and it serves as a sort of marinade, driving flavour.

Hot-Smoked Mackerel

This hot-smoked recipe really is the easiest and fastest way to try dry curing seafood at home for the first time. Hot smoking the mackerel cooks it at the same time it smokes, so really you only need a light curing beforehand. If you were cold smoking the fish instead, you would need a longer curing period to help preserve it and form that impenetrable barrier against bacteria.

Hot smoking is essentially adding wood to a barbecue smoker while gently grilling the fish. I tend to use either apple or oak wood shavings or wood chips for mackerel. Avoid overcooking the fish and always start with light smoke rather than getting carried away and adding too many wood shavings/chips – it's far better for the mackerel to taste of a delicate wood smoke rather than of a bonfire that got out of hand!

Serves 2

2 line-caught mackerel fillets (skin-on)

For the cure

2 tbsp sea salt

1 tbsp light soft brown sugar

Grated zest of 1 lemon

1 tsp hot horseradish sauce

1 tsp coriander seeds, crushed

½ tsp yellow mustard seeds

Start by mixing all the cure ingredients together in a bowl, then rub the cure mix into the mackerel fillets to cover them evenly. Place in a shallow dish and leave them to cure (uncovered) in the fridge for 12–24 hours.

Take the mackerel out of the fridge and remove the cure by gently brushing it off under cold running water. Pat the cured fillets dry.

Place the fillets, skin-side down, on a rack and put into a hot smoker or barbecue oven with wood shavings or wood chips generating aromatic smoke at 180–200°C/350–400°F. Hot smoke the fillets for 6–7 minutes until the fish is cooked through and absorbs lots of smoky flavour. Remove and allow to cool before eating.

Smoked mackerel fillets are fantastic with a watercress salad and some rhubarb chutney, or served warm with poached eggs and toast.

Store the smoked fillets in an airtight container in the fridge for up to 1–2 weeks.

Grandpa's Smoked Mackerel Pâté

I've published my grandpa's smoked mackerel pâté recipe before, always remaining true to the original, but this time I've added my own small generational twist, like a good Cornish whisper changing in the breeze. My devilled version is warmed by a hint of cayenne pepper and feathery fronds of dill add a playful lightness to the recipe.

Makes about 280g/10oz; Serves 4

4 hot-smoked mackerel fillets, cooled
2 tbsp crème fraîche
Juice of 1 lemon
1 tsp horseradish sauce
1 tsp chopped dill
½ tsp cracked black pepper
Pinch of cayenne pepper

Remove the skin from the hot-smoked mackerel fillets and then mix with all the other ingredients in a bowl using a fork to form a coarse texture. Adjust the seasonings to taste.

Try serving this pâté with a celeriac and apple remoulade or green tomato chutney, or with crackers.

This pâté will keep in a covered bowl or an airtight container in the fridge for up to 7–10 days.

How to Dry Cure Sardines

Salting sardines, or pilchards as the Cornish call them, has shaped the local landscape where I live. Local beaches and streets bear the names of 'palace' and 'cellar' to indicate they used to be where the oily fish were salted and pressed. There are even huer's huts dotting the coastline where lookouts would shout to the local fishing boats when a shoal was spotted in the bay.

To me, salting sardines is a simple act of time-travel that we can all have a go at. Sardines can be lightly salted to eat in a day or so, or heavily salted to be stored for a long time. I tend to cure my sardines for between 3–5 days if I'm using them in a stew or a sauce and for just 12–24 hours if I'm throwing them under the grill. You can even cure them for 45–60 minutes if you just want a bit more punch to them when cooking.

Serves 2

12 sardine fillets (skin-on)

For the cure
1 tbsp Cornish sea salt flakes
1 tsp golden caster sugar
½ tsp fennel seeds
½ tsp coriander seeds, crushed
½ tsp dried chilli flakes

Mix all the cure ingredients together in a small bowl.

Start by salting the sardine fillets with an even layer of the cure mix for up to 24 hours. To do this, rub them gently all over with the cure mix so you don't damage the small fillets, then leave on an open tray in the fridge. The flesh will darken slightly in colour and they will firm up a little.

Wash off the cure under cold running water, then pat dry with kitchen paper.

Salted sardines are delicious cooked on a barbecue or pickled with a sweet, spicy vinegar.

Store them in an airtight container in the fridge until you are ready to cook them. They will keep in the fridge for up to 1–2 weeks.

Salted Cornish Sardines and Tomato Salad

Some dishes originate in a place rather than from a person. This recipe is a celebration of the history of Cornwall and the quality ingredients still available here today. When it is sardine season out in Mount's Bay, the Newlyn fishing fleet catch plenty of oily sardines. Known as pilchards by the Cornish, sardines are a great sustainable fish option and they respond very well to intense heat under the grill or on the barbecue.

Serves 2

For the grilled sardines

6 dry-cured sardine fillets (skin-on, see page 88)

2 heritage tomatoes, sliced

1 tbsp olive oil

Pinch of cracked black pepper, plus extra to serve

Small pinch of sea salt

2 slices sourdough

For the salad

12 cherry tomatoes, halved

1 tbsp capers in brine or vinegar, drained

1 garlic clove, finely diced

2 tbsp chopped basil

1 tbsp chopped parsley

Handful of watercress

6 pitted black or green olives, sliced

Handful of pink pickled onions, drained

2 tsp red wine vinegar

1 tsp olive oil

Pinch of salt

Preheat the grill or barbecue to high. Place the cured sardine fillets on a baking tray with the sliced tomatoes and drizzle with the olive oil. Season with the black pepper and salt. Grill (skin-side up under a grill, skin-side down on a barbecue) for 3–4 minutes until the skin starts to blister and blacken. Turn halfway through grilling, but avoid moving much when cooking to prevent damaging the skin.

Meanwhile, toast the sourdough and prepare the salad in a large bowl. For the salad, toss the tomatoes, capers, garlic, herbs, watercress and olives with the pickled onions and season to taste with the vinegar, oil and salt. You shouldn't need much oil or salt as the oily salted sardines will perfectly season the dish for you.

Serve the grilled tomatoes and salad on the sourdough toast and top with the grilled sardines. Make sure you pour over the fish oil and tomato juice from the tray and finish with a little more black pepper and a sprinkling of herbs.

(Left) Salted Cornish sardines on a canvas I painted to celebrate the history of salting fish where I live.

How to Cure Curds (Ricotta)

Cooking with homemade ricotta reminds me of how salt craft elevates the most unlikely foods to cloud-adorned heights. There is a ritual magic to the process of adding salt and lemon juice to warm milk and making cheese – the alchemy of the ingredients into something that's so much more than simple curdled milk. With the addition of salt, a ricotta, cottage cheese or, in fact, any curd, transforms into a culinary delight.

Makes about 100g/3½oz ricotta

1 litre/1¾ pints whole milk

25ml/1fl oz lemon juice

Pinch of sea salt, plus an extra small
  pinch for the curds

To make the ricotta cheese, heat the milk in a saucepan over a medium-low heat. Stir and heat until it reaches 93°C/200°F, then remove the pan from the heat and whisk in the lemon juice and a pinch of salt.

   Stir well for a couple of minutes, then leave to separate into curds and whey. After 15–20 minutes, strain off the yellowish-coloured whey using a cheesecloth/muslin-lined sieve and keep the soft curds. Discard the whey. Salt the curds again in the sieve with a small pinch of salt, then pack loosely into a small, perforated mould or ramekin. Leave, uncovered, on a tray in the fridge for 1–2 days to age before use. Once ready, use as required or transfer to an airtight container and store in the fridge for up to 5 days.

Top Tip

Serve salted ricotta with truffle honey, toasted sourdough and a fennel and grapefruit salad for a real treat! The salty sweet flavours, along with the combination of bitter citrus and anise, are entrancing.

Ricotta Cannelloni

Cooking with ricotta requires very particular balance when tasting and, in my view, the quantity of salt you choose to add and the length of time curing in the fridge is the deftness of hand in the magician's trick.

The chard adds metallic tang and earthy notes like the wind instruments in an orchestra. Nutmeg and pepper, garlic and shallot are the percussion with ricotta on strings. A symphony of pasta and cheese.

Serves 4

For the cannelloni

50g/1¾oz salted butter

1 tbsp plain flour

300ml/½ pint whole milk

50g/1¾oz grated Parmesan cheese

50g/1¾oz mozzarella cheese, drained and finely diced

1 tsp Dijon mustard

Pinch *each* of sea salt and cracked black pepper, or to taste

1 egg yolk, beaten

200g/7oz ricotta (see opposite)

12–16 dried cannelloni tubes

225g/8oz ready-made (or homemade) tomato pasta sauce

2 tbsp panko breadcrumbs

½ tsp truffle sea salt

1 tbsp finely chopped parsley

For the rainbow chard

6 rainbow chard leaves, finely sliced

1 shallot, very finely diced

1 tbsp olive oil

½ tsp grated nutmeg

Pinch each of sea salt and cracked black pepper

Squeeze of lemon juice

Preheat the oven to 180°C fan/400°F/gas mark 6.

Start by preparing the rainbow chard. Sauté the chard and shallot in the olive oil with the nutmeg, salt and pepper in a frying pan over a high heat for a few minutes until softened. Finish with a squeeze of lemon and then leave to cool.

For the cannelloni, make a basic béchamel sauce by gently melting the butter in a saucepan and stirring in the flour to form a roux. Cook for a minute or two, stirring, then gradually incorporate the milk, stirring continuously, until the sauce is thickened and smooth. Finish the sauce by melting in both cheeses and adding the mustard and the salt and pepper to taste. Remove from the heat, and while it is cooling, stir in the beaten egg yolk.

Stir the cooled chard mixture into the ricotta. Fill the cannelloni tubes with the chard/ricotta mixture. Pour the tomato pasta sauce into the bottom of an ovenproof casserole dish or baking tin and arrange the stuffed pasta tubes on top of it. Cover with the cheese sauce and sprinkle over the breadcrumbs.

Bake for 30–35 minutes until golden and bubbling.

Season with the truffle sea salt just before serving for an aromatic finish, and garnish with the chopped parsley. This is delicious served with a crunchy, bitter salad or some garlic bread to accompany.

Clam Pasta with Bottarga

Bottarga, as well as Parmesan cheese and anchovies, are to a seasoned chef what brushes and paint are to an artist. Their inherent saltiness are the tools which, with a light touch, can join a dish together, adding depth and perspective.

Bottarga or cured fish roe is normally made from bluefin tuna from Sicily or grey mullet from Sardinia and, in my opinion, is one of the Mediterranean's best-kept secrets.

Serves 2

1 heaped tsp sea salt crystals

1 shallot, finely diced

2 garlic cloves, finely diced

1 tbsp capers in brine or vinegar, drained

2 tbsp olive oil, plus extra for the pasta and drizzling

350g/12oz fresh pappardelle pasta

500g/1lb 2oz live clams (in shell), rinsed (discard any open ones that don't close when tapped sharply)

4 asparagus spears, sliced

Good glug of white wine

4 quarters of Preserved Lemon (see page 96), drained and sliced

2 tbsp chopped flat-leaf parsley

Sea salt crystals and cracked black pepper

2 tbsp grated bottarga, to serve

Season a large pan of water with the measured sea salt crystals and bring to the boil for the pasta.

Meanwhile, in a large sauté pan, soften the shallot, garlic and capers in the measured olive oil over a medium heat for 2–3 minutes.

Add the pasta to the pan of boiling water and cook for 3–4 minutes or until just tender, then drain and toss with a little olive oil.

While the pasta is cooking, add the clams and asparagus to the sauté pan along with the white wine. Cover the pan with a lid and steam over a high heat for 3–4 minutes until all the clams are open (fish out and discard any that haven't opened).

Add the preserved lemon and parsley to the clams. Stir well and season with a small pinch of salt and some black pepper. You don't need much salt as the cured roe will do the majority of the seasoning in this dish.

Add the cooked pasta to the pan and toss gently, adding a little more olive oil if required.

Remove from the heat and serve with an extremely generous covering of grated bottarga.

> ### Try This
>
> *Serve grated bottarga on toasted ciabatta with olive oil and lemon juice, or shaved onto a steak tartare. Also excellent with pickled beetroot and pumpernickel.*

How to Cure Egg Yolks

Free-range egg yolks are full of an incredible array of metallic, umami, herby and quietly pronounced flavours that need little doing to them to steal the show on a plate. Yet a perfectly poached egg on toasted sourdough truly comes alive with a pinch of sea salt sprinkled over the sunshine yolk. The simple addition of salt takes the hearty egg flavour and elevates it to the heights of luxury.

I've been curing egg yolks for years and I love the way you not only add flavour but radically alter the texture, creating another unique and versatile ingredient in the process.

Try grating cured egg yolk on hot pasta or risotto or adding it to a Caesar salad instead of anchovies to season. Thinly slice cured egg yolk and serve on toast with some pickled beetroot and caraway seeds for a mind-blowingly tasty brunch.

Makes 6 cured egg yolks

125g/4½oz sea salt – try a blend
  with cracked peppercorns
40g/1½oz caster sugar
6 free-range egg yolks

To cure the egg yolks, simply mix the salt and sugar together in a small glass tray. Use a whole egg (in shell) to make six shallow indentations in the surface of the curing salt and then carefully lay the egg yolks onto the curing salt in these dips. Sprinkle the tops with any remaining curing salt from the gaps around the eggs, then cover and place in the fridge. Leave for 5–7 days. Turn every couple of days for an even texture. The water will slowly drain from the egg yolks as they cure and be absorbed into the surrounding salt, and the yolks will quickly feel slightly tacky but firm to the touch.

When the cured yolks are ready, gently brush off the excess salt cure with a pastry brush. Store the cured yolks in a sealed container in the fridge for up to 2–3 weeks. If using them immediately for the Cured Egg Carbonara recipe (see page 95), open-freeze the cured yolks on a small tray for 30 minutes to help when grating them over the finished pasta.

Cured Egg Carbonara

This carbonara recipe takes time to prepare in advance but only takes moments to cook. It's a real crowd-pleaser, and don't be shy with the pepper, too. The greatest carbonara of my life was in Rome in an incredibly picturesque area called *Trastevere*. After a very long walk following a guidebook map with the obligatory espresso stops to ask for directions, we arrived in this magical Roman district with its bustling streets and vibrant restaurant scene. We found a place to eat on the edge of a gorgeous square and ordered carbonara with more pepper than I'd ever seen on one plate. This dish was a revelation on how to season. The pepper worked with the salty pancetta and Parmesan in perfect balance.

Serves 2

250g/9oz dried rigatoni pasta

6 slices pancetta, diced

2 garlic cloves, finely sliced

1 tsp olive oil

2 egg yolks

55g/2oz grated Parmesan cheese

1–2 tsp cracked black pepper

1 cured egg yolk (see page 93), grated

Sea salt

To make a classic carbonara, cook the pasta in a large saucepan of heavily salted boiling water according to the packet instructions until al dente.

About 5 minutes or so before the pasta is ready, in a separate saucepan, fry the pancetta and garlic with the olive oil over a medium-high heat for 5–6 minutes until the pancetta starts to caramelise. Whisk the egg yolks and Parmesan together and add to the saucepan. At this point, remove the pan from the heat and stir vigorously to stop the sauce from curdling. Add a small ladleful of pasta cooking water and keep stirring. Gradually add another ladleful or so of the pasta water, stirring the whole time until the carbonara sauce forms a rich, velvety texture.

At this point, use a slotted spoon to drain and add the cooked pasta, then season with the cracked black pepper. Serve with plenty of grated cured egg yolk over the top of the pasta for a delicious, golden seasoning.

Try This

If you enjoy cured egg yolks, then try brining boiled eggs with gently cracked shells in soy sauce or miso for an umami-packed version that results in a decorative marbled effect. It can also be great fun to pickle eggs in a sweet and salty vinegar solution with beetroot for a brightly coloured pink egg.

How to Make Preserved Lemons

I confess I'm barmy about preserved lemon. To me, it's sunshine in a jar. The complex flavours work in perfect unison and I find it enhances so much of my cookery from seafood recipes to barbecued chicken, to a good tabbouleh or a lush risotto. My version uses smoked sea salt, rose petals and cardamom to capture what I love about summer – the blend of smoky barbecues wafting in the garden haze, aromatic spices and flowers in bloom.

Makes 1 x 1 litre/1¾ pint jar

8 unwaxed lemons

150g/5½oz smoked sea salt
  (see *Salt Geek* below)

6–8 green cardamom pods, crushed

½ tsp dried rose petals

½ tsp smoked dried chilli flakes

To make the preserved lemons, start by sterilising a large (1 litre/1¾ pint) glass jar (with lid). Preheat the oven to 150°C fan/340°F/gas mark 3½. Wash and rinse the jar and lid, place in the oven on a shelf and heat for 15 minutes. Allow to cool.

Slice the lemons lengthways into quarters and place on a chopping board. In a small bowl, mix together the smoked salt, cardamom pods, rose petals and chilli flakes. Sprinkle some of this salt blend all over the lemon quarters, then rub another small handful of the salt blend into the cut-sides of the lemon quarters.

Pack the lemon quarters into the sterilised jar, sprinkling a little more of the remaining salt blend over each layer as you go, pressing all the salted lemon segments into the jar, then tightly secure the lid in place. Leave the lemons to cure in their brine in the sealed jar in a cool, dry place for 2–3 months, turning the jar occasionally.

Once ready, drain and use the preserved lemons as required. Once opened, store the jar in the fridge and use within 1 month.

Salt Geek

Cold-smoked sea salt provides a woody, umami profile to the preserved lemons. For this recipe, I use Cornish sea salt that's been smoked over cherry, apple and green oak wood for 48 hours. It's not an overpowering salt and I find the aroma delicate enough to add complexity while not masking the lemon.

Minted Pea Risotto

This risotto is inspired by the meal my wife and I created to serve at our wedding. The inclusion of turmeric is new, though, and the slight smoky tone from the lemons is a good adaptation which I hope you enjoy.

Serves 2

½ shallot, finely diced

55g/2oz Smoked Butter (see page 223)
   or 2 tbsp olive oil

1 tsp garlic purée

150g/5½oz risotto rice

½ tsp ground turmeric

Splash of white wine

500ml/18fl oz hot vegetable stock

85g/3oz podded fresh garden peas
   or frozen peas

1 tbsp chopped mint, plus extra
   to garnish

4 quarters of Preserved Lemon (see
   page 96), drained and finely sliced

1 tbsp soft goats' cheese

Pinch of Smoked Sea Salt
   (see page 216)

Pinch of cracked black pepper

Sea salt

Make this risotto in the usual manner by first softening the shallot in the smoked butter or olive oil in a saucepan over a medium heat, then adding the garlic purée, rice and turmeric. After 1–2 minutes, add the wine to deglaze the pan, then reduce the wine for 2–3 minutes. Pour a ladleful of the hot vegetable stock into the pan, then repeat once it has been absorbed by the rice, stirring regularly. Continue in this way, gradually adding the remaining stock and cooking the risotto over a low heat, until all the stock has been added, about 15–20 minutes.

Meanwhile, blanch the fresh peas in a separate small pan of salted water for 1–2 minutes, then refresh in a bowl of iced water and drain. Frozen peas won't need blanching.

Finish the risotto by mixing in the peas, mint, preserved lemon and soft cheese. Bring back to a simmer and check the rice for a cooked but slightly nutty texture before serving. Season to taste with the smoked salt and black pepper and serve with extra mint sprinkled on top to garnish.

Seasoning your food can be done dry with a pinch here and there, a sprinkle of some crystals or a flick of some flakes, or you can choose to season with a salty or briny solution. Whereas dry curing is all about harnessing salt's osmosis powers, wet curing relies more on the power of diffusion. Diffusion is the movement of salts from an area of high concentration to an area of low concentration in solution until they reach equilibrium. Visually, you can easily observe osmosis when you sprinkle cut cucumber with salt – after a few minutes, you can see the water glistening on its surface as it is drawn out from within. Diffusion is invisible to the naked eye but is just as miraculous.

Wet curing is similar to the marinating process but works without acid. Meat, fish or vegetables are immersed in a strong brine solution, which draws out moisture from the food via osmosis and preserves it. At the same time, the salts, herbs and spices in the brine penetrate the food to impart bucket-loads of salty flavour by diffusion, while the liquid in the brine prevents dehydration, keeping the meat moist and juicy with a butter-soft texture.

How it Works

Salt dissolved in solution has the ability to season food from the inside. When you fully submerge food in a brine, it creates an anaerobic environment that is perfect for either preserving or simply seasoning your ingredients. Firstly, salt dissolved in the brine draws moisture out from the microbes that may be present via osmosis and kills them (just like in the process of dry curing), but secondly, the lack of oxygen also prevents oxidation and discolouration of your food.

When the moisture is drawn out of cells using dry curing as a method, it can concentrate the flavour but also dehydrate your food. The added benefit of wet curing, however, is that you are not simply drying out your ingredients. Instead, as the salts dissolve in water, the electrolytes or ions penetrate deeper into meat membranes, even in larger cuts of meat and whole birds. This process of diffusion also

prevents an uneven cure where some areas could be salted and others not. I almost always add sugar to my brines as a counterweight to the saltiness, and this also encourages the development of *Lactobacillus*, which is a beneficial bacteria that helps both flavour and preservation. A sweet brine is ideal to cure and ferment whole vegetables for 4–5 days before cooking.

Diffusion

Diffusion simultaneously tenderises and keeps food moist, so it's a salt skill that's worth mastering, but salt is slow to diffuse. The process of diffusion whereby salt moves from an area of high concentration to a less salty environment as it passes through cells is a slower process than osmosis. It will eventually be evenly distributed – thus seasoning food from within – so allow yourself time for the salt to travel to the centre of larger foods.

It also works better at room temperature. Try to get into the habit of taking foods out of the fridge for an hour or so before you cook them, but while they are still brining, to allow them time to diffuse while the meat/food relaxes. The movement of salt from an area of high concentration to low during diffusion also results in equilibrium, achieving an even salinity throughout – in other words, perfectly seasoned ingredients from the inside and out.

The Power of Salted Water

I predict that purified seawater is the future of cooking. Italians swear by salty pasta water at nearly 3.5 per cent salinity and I have cooked some delicious food in seawater – it's the ultimate natural brine. That said, I wouldn't recommend cooking with seawater regularly unless you are 100 per cent sure it's clean and safe.

Moist and Juicy

Salt has a remarkable ability to keep cells hydrated and helps prevent food from drying out while cooking. With an ingredient like meat, which is about 70 per cent water, around 30 per cent of a protein's moisture can be lost during cooking if you are not careful. However, salt used in a wet cure also keeps food juicy when cooked by increasing the water-holding capacity of its cells. This is why our bodies rely on sodium and it is so important to our hydration levels when exercising or sweating. When cooking something like a whole brined chicken, the dissolved salt ions that make their way into the centre of the bird through diffusion and bind the water in the muscle fibres more tightly together, help to resist the shrinkage that ordinarily squeezes juice out when cooked. The salt also conducts the heat smoothly, allowing for an even texture throughout.

In a concentrated brine, the salt also helps to dissolve the tough proteins in meat, resulting in a juicy, tenderised texture that's moist and softer to eat. If you salt for longer than 24 hours in a strong concentrated brine, however, instead of diffusion you will start drawing too much moisture out of the food, as the food will become saturated with as much salt as the cells can retain, so that the moisture is drawn out into the salty brine solution in an attempt to reach equilibrium. This risks ending up removing too much water, leaving you with dry, salty food rather than juicy well-seasoned ingredients.

(Opposite) The Buttermilk Fried Chicken process (see page 108).

Wet Curing Top Tips

You will need a non-reactive container to seal the solution and the meat while curing. The easiest option is to use a large, brining bag. A brining bag is a useful bit of kit to buy for larger food items. It is a resealable polythene food bag that's easy to lay on a tray, providing an easy way to brine in the fridge. For an even larger cut of meat or whole fish, you may need to use an ice-box (cool box), wash-tub or even a plastic bin (if this won't fit in your fridge, add ice to the brine solution instead of water). Keep food submerged and refrigerated below 5°C/41°F at all times, so top up regularly with more ice and keep checking the temperature with a thermometer. Remove from the fridge (but keep the food in the brine) for the last hour to return it to room temperature before cooking.

Don't reuse brine solutions, and always use a solution of at least 4 per cent salt – but beyond 8 per cent and the meat may become unpalatable. Change the solution daily if curing a large cut of meat.

A technical way to measure the strength of your brine is to use a salinometer or brinometer, which consist of a float with a stem attached. The reading is taken at the level the stem floats in the brine.

To reduce the saltiness of brined ingredients, soak them in fresh water for 1 hour after the wet-curing stage and before cooking.

How to Make Salt Beef

My recipe is a blend of both Irish corned beef and a Jewish-style salt beef used for amazing pastrami sandwiches – the starting point for both is fairly similar. I love the subtle spiced flavour that you get roasting the beef low and slow for a wholesome meat that's delicious cold in sandwiches or served warm with vegetables as a main meal. After it's been brined and drained, try cooking your salt beef in stout with onions for a decadent dish or smoking it on the barbecue with hickory wood chips for a pastrami.

With a brisket, the iconic pink-coloured flesh is always the result of the chosen cure. I hardly ever use pink salt for curing due to the nitrates, but I wanted to show how to use it in a recipe, as it's still the salt of choice for the majority of butchery and charcuterie businesses. The pink colour is retained – when you only use sea salts for dry curing and brining meats, the meat can appear greyer. There are health risks associated with consuming too many nitrates and generally I avoid them, but it's completely your choice.

Serves 8

25g/1oz Prague Powder #1

2–4kg/4lb 8oz–8lb 13oz beef brisket

2 sprigs rosemary

2 sprigs bay

2 sprigs thyme

4 star anise

1 tsp *each* black, green and white peppercorns

1 tsp coriander seeds

1 tsp yellow mustard seeds

1 tsp caraway seeds

1 tsp dried chilli flakes

Dissolve the pink curing salt (Prague Powder #1) in 3 litres/5¼ pints of water in a large plastic container (or another suitable container – see Wet Curing Top Tips on page 102) by whisking them together. Submerge the beef brisket in the salted water, along with all the herbs and spices. Cover and keep refrigerated below 5°C/41°F and turn daily.

Leave to brine for 5–7 days.

Remove the brisket from the brine and pat dry. Discard the brining solution and flavourings.

To cook the cured beef, preheat the oven to 150°C fan/340°F/gas mark 3½. Place the cured beef in a large roasting tray with 1 litre/1¾ pints of water and cover with foil. Slow roast for 6 hours for a smaller joint and for up to 8 hours for larger briskets for best results.

Allow to rest, covered with foil, for 15–20 minutes, then slice and serve warm, or serve cold. Serve with rye bread, mustard, Swiss cheese and sauerkraut.

Store the cooled salt beef in an airtight container in the fridge for up to 10 days, and slice as needed.

Cider-brined Chicken

Juicy, sweet, gently spiced brined chicken is a marvel of home cookery. I love brining chicken as it makes for great results when cooking and it's a key part of learning to pre-season. By salting well in advance, a chicken can remain moister when cooked and absorb buckets of flavour. Generally, you can apply a 7 per cent rule for brining – so for every 1 litre/1¾ pints of water, add 70g/2½oz of salt. For larger foods like turkey, whole chickens and cuts of pork, you can reduce this to 5 per cent salinity. I'm not sure what I prefer best – cider-brined chicken or buttermilk-brined wings (see page 108). Try both and choose your favourite.

Serves 6

2kg/4lb 8oz oven-ready free-range
  chicken, giblets removed

For the 5 per cent brine
125g/4½oz salt crystals
70g/2½oz caster sugar
500ml/18fl oz dry cider
Knob of root ginger
4 garlic cloves, whole
4 sprigs rosemary
4 sprigs thyme
4 dried juniper berries
2 green cardamom pods,
  lightly crushed
2 sticks lemongrass, cut into thirds
  or bruised
1 tsp yellow mustard seeds
1 tsp dried green peppercorns
1 tsp black peppercorns
1 tsp coriander seeds

To roast
½ lemon
1 whole brined chicken (from above)
1 red onion, roughly chopped
4 chorizo sausages, sliced into coins
6 Chantenay carrots, chopped
Sieved brining herbs and spices
  (from above)
2 tbsp olive oil

For the chimichurri
Large bunch of mint
Large bunch of parsley
4 tbsp olive oil
2 tbsp red wine vinegar
4 garlic cloves, peeled
½ red pepper, de-seeded and diced
1 red chilli, de-seeded and
  finely chopped
½ tsp cumin seeds
Sea salt and cracked black pepper

Make the brine in a large jug – whisk 4.5 litres/8 pints of water with the salt and sugar until they have dissolved. Add the cider and all of aromatics and spices.

Using a large brining bag (see page 102), submerge the whole chicken in the brine, seal the bag and place in the fridge below 5°C/41°F. Leave to brine for 24 hours and then turn. Brine for a further 24 hours.

Preheat the oven to 180°C fan/400°F/gas mark 6.

Pour away the brine using a sieve, but keep the aromatic ingredients to flavour the chicken when roasting. Place the lemon half in the chicken cavity, then lay the chicken on a trivet of the onion, chorizo and carrots in a roasting tin. Sprinkle with half the reserved herbs and spices (discard the rest). Drizzle with the oil and roast for 45 minutes or until the chicken is cooked through and the internal temperature is above 73°C/163°F. Allow to rest, covered with foil, for 15 minutes before carving.

While the chicken rests, make a quick chimichurri sauce by simply blitzing all the ingredients together in a food processor until smooth, then seasoning to taste with salt and pepper.

Serve the chicken with baked sweet potato chips/wedges and the roasted vegetables and chorizo, with the chimichurri drizzled over the top.

Buttermilk Fried Chicken

Most brines are salts dissolved in water, but if you use buttermilk instead, you can coax out the most wonderful creamy, tangy and uber-moist flavours in chicken. This recipe works like a dream and is the only way to cook wings.

Serves 8

1kg/2lb 4oz free-range chicken wings

500ml/18fl oz buttermilk

55g/2oz Smoked Sea Salt (see page 216)

4 tbsp plain flour, seasoned with a pinch *each* of sea salt and cracked black pepper

1 litre/1¾ pints vegetable oil, for frying

For the spice blend

1 tbsp paprika

1 tsp garlic powder

1 tsp onion powder

1 tsp mild chilli powder

1 tsp dried sage

1 tsp dried thyme

1 tsp ground white pepper

½ tsp dried chilli flakes

Mix together all the ingredients for the spice blend in a small bowl. Store in an airtight container if making in advance or creating a larger batch. This blend will keep in the store cupboard for up to 2–3 months.

I like to mix my chicken wings, buttermilk, smoked salt and 2 tablespoons of the spice blend together in a large bowl. Cover and then leave to brine in the fridge below 5°C/41°F for 12–24 hours to tenderise and work its magic.

The next day, remove the chicken wings from the buttermilk brine (discard the brine) and dredge on a tray with the seasoned flour and the remaining spice blend to coat.

Heat the oil in a large, deep, heavy-based saucepan over a medium heat to 180°C/350°F (or until a small piece of bread dropped in browns within 30 seconds), then deep-fry the wings (in batches) for 8–10 minutes until cooked, golden and crispy on the outside and succulent inside. Bring the oil back up to temperature before adding each batch.

Remove the wings using a slotted spoon and drain on kitchen paper to remove the excess oil. This is properly seasoned fried chicken that's delicious served hot with slaw and some hot pepper sauce.

(Right) Buttermilk fried chicken seasoned with smoked sea salt and rosemary flowers.

How to Cure a Ham

Curing my own ham is a well-established festive tradition in the Strawbridge household; tucking into a clove-studded ham on Christmas morning is a real highlight for me. In fact, over the years, I've gradually incorporated making hams across more of the year to bring that same level of comfort and homely appreciation for the simple things. I'd even go so far as to say that for me, making a ham captures an instinctive ebb and flow of the seasons, mimicking the tides with highs and lows, reflecting times of both plenty and of scarcity, and the importance of preserving a nourishing larder. Salt craft at its assured best – a friend for all seasons.

The wet-curing process is still a form of dehydration that draws moisture out of the food and makes it an inhospitable environment for bacteria to degrade the meat. You can also dry cure hams, and I have had some great results producing a Parma-style dry-cured leg of ham over the years – an entire leg packed in a barrel of salt that's then wrapped in muslin and air-dried for 12–24 months. However, I've always found it costly – requiring huge volumes of salt, space and time. So personally, I prefer to wet cure my hams in a sweet brine. I choose to add a little amount of nitrates to keep an attractive pink colour in the cured meat and to soften the salty brine with a sweetness and hint of spice.

Makes 1 large ham/Serves 4–6

1 boned unsmoked gammon joint, weighing about 1.5–2kg/ 3lb 5oz–4lb 8oz

For the brine

160g/5¾oz sea salt

500g/1lb 2oz golden caster sugar

25g/1oz Prague Powder #1 (optional)

2 star anise

1 cinnamon stick

1 tsp fennel seeds

1 tsp black mustard seeds

1 tsp dried juniper berries

½ tsp dried chilli flakes

Place all the brine ingredients in a large saucepan with 2 litres/3½ pints of water and heat until the salt and sugar dissolve, then allow to cool. Place in a non-reactive brining tub or a large brining bag (see page 102) with the gammon joint. Ensure the joint is submerged and cover the tub, or reseal the bag and place it on a tray.

Leave to brine in the fridge below 5°C/41°F for 3 days per 1kg/2lb 4oz.

To boil the cured ham, strain the brine, reserving the spices (discard the brine), then add the spices, leek, shallot, garlic and herbs to a large saucepan. Add the ham and cover with enough water to ensure it remains covered while cooking. Bring to a gentle simmer, then slow cook for 3–4 hours or until you can easily slide a skewer into the centre of the joint. You may need to top up with more water as it evaporates to keep the ham submerged while simmering. Taste the cooking water halfway through cooking and if it's too salty, replace half of the water with fresh boiling water and return to the stove.

Once cooked, allow the ham to rest in the cooking water until it is cool enough to handle (or see opposite, if roasting it), then drain and air dry on a rack in the fridge (with a tray underneath) for 24 hours.

You can now serve this cold as a delicious, boiled ham, but I love

1 leek, roughly chopped

1 shallot, halved

1 bulb garlic, cloves separated,
    peeled and cut in half

1 fresh bouquet garni

To roast the ham (optional)

1 tbsp rough-cut orange marmalade

1 tbsp runny honey

1 tsp wholegrain mustard

½ tsp English mustard powder

going the extra mile and roasting my ham for an extra layer of umami sweetness on the palate.

To roast the ham, preheat the oven to 180°C fan/400°F/gas mark 6.

In a small saucepan, heat together the marmalade, honey and both types of mustard over a medium-low heat for 4–5 minutes, stirring continuously, until it starts to bubble and thicken slightly. Using a pastry brush, glaze the entire boiled ham (while it is still hot), then place in a roasting tray and roast for 25–30 minutes. Repeat the glazing every 10–15 minutes for an even coverage and glossy finish.

Carve the hot or cold ham into slices to serve. Served warm, it is delicious with wilted kale, fried eggs and chips, or try it cold with a ploughman's or sliced in a croque monsieur.

The cooked ham will keep, wrapped in foil, in the fridge for up to 10 days. Carve off slices as needed.

A Cornish Ploughman's

I find there's nothing that celebrates slow food quite as much as taking a joint
of rare-breed pork and transforming it into decadent sliced, sweet, spiced ham
– guaranteed to steal the show on any lunch platter and at the heart of a rustic
ploughman's. This is humble food that takes honest hard work and patience
to prepare. With that extra effort comes a rewarding satisfaction
and pride that you taste on the plate.

This cold cured ham works really well served with robust spiced chutney,
mature Cheddar cheese and tart pickles to complement its bittersweet,
marmalade glaze.

Serves 4

4–8 slices ham (see cured ham
  recipe on pages 110–11)
150g/5½oz mature Cheddar cheese,
  sliced (at room temperature)
4 pickled onions, drained
4 tsp farmhouse or seasonal chutney
  (of your choice)
4 tsp piccalilli
1 apple, sliced
1 tomato, sliced
1 stick of celery, sliced into chunks
Salad leaves or edible flowers,
  to garnish
Sliced rustic bread or crackers,
  to serve

Slice the roasted ham once it has cooled (see page 111).

Serve the ploughman's on a large sharing platter or wooden board for
people to help themselves. Serve the ham and cheese slices with the
pickled onions, chutney, piccalilli, apple, tomato and celery alongside.

Garnish with some salad leaves or edible flowers and serve with rustic
bread or crackers.

How to Pickle Herring

The herring is from the same family of fish as the sardine, and they are a fish that shoals in their thousands. The small, oily fish travel from colder deep-water seas to warmer coastal spawning sites and can disappear just as quickly. Fishermen seeking to preserve the fish on long voyages quickly discovered there was no need to dry cure herring or air dry them. Instead, herring could be brined and pickled with a salty-sweet vinegar.

Herring are very rich in vitamin D3 and omega-3 and deliver barrel-loads of flavour. My recipe souses the fish in vinegar to give a layer of sweet, acidic tang to the flavour. It also provides the additional benefit of heat that gently cooks the fillets, providing you with peace of mind when curing. You could opt to brine in a 20 per cent salinity solution using the traditional method of wet curing with water, and then, once cured, transfer to an acidic sweet pickle for flavour, however, my method makes it quick and easy to add flavour and season from the inside out in just one process.

Serves 2

For the pickled herring
150ml/¼ pint red wine vinegar
50ml/2fl oz boiling water
25g/1oz golden caster sugar
15g/½oz sea salt (see Salt
   Choice opposite)
1 shallot, finely diced
2 allspice berries
1 tsp ground sumac
½ tsp dried red pepper flakes
½ tsp black peppercorns
2 bay leaves
2 herring fillets, skin removed
   (about 320g/11½oz total weight)

To serve and garnish
Sour pickles
Radishes
Potato salad
Hard-boiled eggs
Sourdough crispbreads
Sprigs dill

For the pickled herring, gently heat the vinegar in a small saucepan with the hot water, sugar, salt, shallot, all the spices and the bay leaves, stirring until dissolved, then bring gently to the boil. Generally, when pickling fish in this way, aim for a brine that's between 10–15 per cent – I'm keeping my salinity lower here because I'm using vinegar in the recipe, too.

Take the pan off the heat when it starts to boil and allow to cool for 5–10 minutes. Pour this over the herring fillets in a suitable container, submerging the fillets to allow them to cure. If the cure is too hot when you pour it, then the herring will end up softer. I wait until it is comfortable to touch at around the drinking temperature of a cup of coffee (about 65°C/150°F).

Cool, cover the container, then leave the herring to cure in the fridge below 5°C/41°F for 2–3 days.

Once ready, you can soak the herring to reduce the saltiness before serving. If you want to do this, strain off the wet cure and leave the fillets in ice-cold water for 1–2 hours, then drain. Personally, I enjoy a pickled herring that has an intense sweet and salty flavour to then pair with creamy and acidic condiments.

Try serving the pickled herring with sour pickles, radishes, potato salad, hard-boiled eggs and sourdough crispbreads. Garnish with sprigs of fresh dill.

Havsno

 For this recipe, I wanted to pair the herring with a Norwegian salt. To me, *Havsno* has a sea beet metallic tang, with caper lightness and a sweet finish. Fine crystals that dissolve in brine carrying sea mineral flavours, pair perfectly with the sumac, red pepper flakes, peppercorns and sharp shallot. *Havsno* is a hand-harvested salt that means 'snow of the sea'. It's produced from 100 per cent renewable and clean hydro energy, revitalising the sea salt production in Norway and crystallising the clean northern seas.

A Rainbow Pickled Veg Plate

Rainbows spring to mind when you see this on the plate – the pot of gold is realising just how simple these are to make...

Salting vegetables draws out some of their moisture and leaves them ready to draw back in your culinary breath – the calming process of osmosis in action like a yoga class breathing pattern. A slice of cucumber or a ribbon of beetroot can keep its crunch after salting while soaking in the flavours of your choice, immersed in a so-sweet pickling bath. It's intoxicating when you start pickling salted vegetables yourself. They provide a kaleidoscope of colours – the entire colour wheel – along with high-frequency tastes, textures coming alive as you bite and the seasoning poised and beaming, shining through blinding rays of delicate primary light.

Serves 6 (all the pickled veg together)

2 tbsp fine Himalayan crystal salt

For the carrots
6 baby carrots, peeled
150ml/¼ pint mirin
1 tbsp caster sugar
1 tsp shichimi togarashi (a Japanese
  seven-spice blend)

For the cauliflower
¼ cauliflower, broken into florets
150ml/¼ pint white wine vinegar
1 tbsp caster sugar
2 tbsp sliced (peeled) fresh
  turmeric root
1 tsp fenugreek seeds
1 tsp coriander seeds
½ tsp dried chilli flakes

For the beetroot
2 beetroots, peeled and thinly sliced
150ml/¼ pint red wine vinegar
2 tbsp light soft brown sugar
1 tsp za'atar

Slice all the vegetables thinly and uniformly so that they cure and pickle at a similar rate to each other, except leave the carrots whole and the cauliflower broken into florets. Arrange on a large plastic tray (keeping the different veg separate from each other) and sprinkle evenly with the fine Himalayan salt. Leave for at least 1–2 hours at room temperature or overnight in the fridge below 5°C/41°F.

Prepare all the pickling solutions, one at a time (rinse the pan out between making each solution). In a small saucepan, heat the vinegar and sugar with the corresponding spices until the sugar dissolves and the mixture comes to the boil. Transfer each of the salted vegetables into separate small bowls, then pour over the matching hot pickling solution.

Toss each veg in its pickling solution to coat evenly and then leave submerged to cool back to room temperature, stirring each bowlful of veg every 5 minutes. Remove each veg from its pickling solution using a slotted spoon while the veg still has a bit of bite and before it softens too much. Discard the pickling solution, aromatics and spices before serving.

Serve all the pickled veg as a colourful side at a barbecue or as a starter with a cooling labneh dip.

Once drained off, these pickled vegetables will all keep together in a sealed container in the fridge for up to 2–3 weeks.

For the radishes

6 radishes, finely sliced

150ml/¼ pint cider vinegar

1 tbsp caster sugar

4 garlic cloves, sliced

1 jalapeño chilli pepper, de-seeded
   and sliced

Pinch of dried chilli flakes

For the cucumber

1 cucumber, crinkle-cut using a retro
   slicer, or sliced into thin discs

150ml/¼ pint cider vinegar

1 tbsp caster sugar

2 bay leaves

1 tbsp chopped dill

1 tsp yellow mustard seeds

For the red cabbage

¼ red cabbage, finely sliced

150ml/¼ pint sherry vinegar

1 tbsp light soft brown sugar

1 tsp wholegrain mustard

1 sprig rosemary

For the onions

2 red onions, finely sliced

150ml/¼ pint cider vinegar

1 tbsp caster sugar

1 tsp ground sumac

The Full Works Sauce

I spent my school years growing up in Malvern, Worcestershire. There were three things from the local area that I was immensely proud of: spring water that gushed from the hills, cold and bright; the local Morgan car factory churning out handmade, exquisitely lined cars that I imagined one day I would drive (I'd be so lucky?!); and the famous Worcestershire Sauce.

My Full Works Sauce tastes of a hedgerow rumble or a driving blues rhythm. I find it sweet, spicy, savoury, salty and umami all at the same time. Make this recipe your own and experiment by adding other umami-rich ingredients like black garlic or roasted onions and your own spicing to turn up the volume in your own way. You can then use this sauce in pretty much everything, including pasta sauces and stews, in barbecue mops and glazes, for seasoning grilled vegetables, and with every cheese toastie from now onwards. This sauce takes cheese on toast to the next level – with only a few drops, you can transform a cheese toastie and reveal hidden flavours which explode under a hot grill.

Serves 4

6 tinned anchovy fillets, with oil
    from the tin
1 onion, finely diced
200g/7oz mushrooms, diced
1 tbsp grated (peeled) root ginger
1 tsp smoked garlic paste
2 tbsp date molasses
1 tbsp dark soft brown sugar
100ml/3½fl oz malt vinegar
50ml/2fl oz dark soy sauce
50ml/2fl oz tamari
2 tsp tamarind paste
2 cinnamon sticks
1 tsp dried chipotle chilli flakes

Add the anchovies, onion and mushrooms to a saucepan and gently start to sauté them in the oil from the fish over a medium-low heat. This will build some depth of flavour at this stage for a more full-bodied sauce later. Cook gently until the mushrooms start to brown a little, then add the ginger and garlic.

Next, stir in the molasses and sugar. Allow to melt, then bubble for 1–2 minutes, but don't let it burn. Add the vinegar, soy, tamari and tamarind, plus the cinnamon sticks and chilli flakes. Reduce the heat a little further and bubble on a low simmer for 15–20 minutes, stirring occasionally.

Strain the sauce (see below) into a sterilised bottle, seal and allow to cool. Keep in the fridge, unopened, for up to 4–6 weeks. Once opened, store in the fridge and use within 10 days.

Use the leftover paste of mushrooms and spices to make an umami-packed ketchup by removing the cinnamon sticks and blitzing the rest in a food processor until smooth. The mushroom ketchup is excellent with roast potato wedges, cauliflower steaks or fondant celeriac. Store this umami condiment in a sterilised jar in the fridge for up to 1 month.

Chapter Eleven
Lacto-Ferments

Sour pickling is a traditional form of salt craft that blows my mind. There are some fantastic books out there, anything by Sandor Katz or Pascal Bauder is a great starting point. I've read and written extensively on this subject myself and it continues to amaze me how the possibilities are endless.

To truly appreciate these two tastes together, you need only taste some sauerkraut with a rye cracker or bite into a sour pickled dill cucumber to know exactly what I'm talking about. I would honestly say that nowhere in food does salt make such a profound difference to taste as when it's paired with sour. It's a daredevil taste challenge, not a subtle one – it throws you over Niagara Falls in a salty pickle barrel and gives you one hell of a ride. You feel like your face has just been sprayed with an intense briny splash of bittersweet wave and as you lick your lips, there's a sour sunshine tang which reminds you that you are still alive and having a whale of a time.

Before we get started, I want to quickly share an epiphany I had several years back when it all slotted together to make sense. I realised that, yes, you need to follow a rigid process, but, in fact, we're not in charge because it is not about cooking; it is about providing the environment for flavour to thrive and giving the ingredients the time to cook for you.

Fermentation isn't rocket science, but it does require some accuracy for best results. With a little care and attention and controlling the exact percentage of salt added to food, you can delicately balance the growth of beneficial bacteria and develop incredible lactic tang flavour, while simultaneously preventing the growth of unwanted bacteria. I find this remarkable every single time I ferment something. It is a simple case of providing the right conditions for flavour to flourish. If you provide your ferment with the correct amount of salt in a clean, anaerobic environment, then it will radically change flavour while you sit back and watch the bubbles rise before your eyes.

How it Works

Lacto-fermentation transforms vegetables and fruit with tangy, fizzing, gut-friendly bacteria. The sour pickles extend the shelf life and are unique in the way they blend salty and sour together as tastes to appreciate. The beneficial bacteria in a ferment consume glucose from the vegetables and fruit; they then convert this into lactic acid. As part of this partial breakdown of plant sugars, we get an acidic by-product that creates delicious flavours. Salt is instrumental in this process and the end product retains a well-seasoned balance – enhanced further by the symbiotic sour taste.

The process of lacto-fermentation is simple to explain but is astoundingly complex in terms of results. The level of salt added to a vegetable controls the performance of the flavours like an effects pedal for a musician. Osmosis is another natural process key to sour pickling: the propensity of water to penetrate a permeable barrier, in order to balance out the concentration of chemicals dissolved either side of the barrier. By rubbing salt over vegetables and fruit, water is drawn out and salt is drawn in, until the amount of salt dissolved is equal inside and out. The liquid produced is often enough (once the ingredients are packed into a jar) to create the anaerobic environment beloved of lacto-bacteria – so don't throw it away! A warm environment helps speed up the fermentation process of 7–10 days. Lower temperatures lead to a slower rate of fermentation to my taste, creating deeper, more full-bodied ferment flavours. The acidic, salty and oxygen-free environment inhibits unwanted bacteria and moulds, so you should be able to store the sealed ferments at room temperature for several months.

Sauerkraut

There are few things as satisfying as the moment when you massage cabbage leaves with salt and burst the cells, releasing moisture that starts to swill in the bowl as a fresh brine mixed with vegetal goodness.

Sauerkraut involves thinly slicing cabbage and massaging salt into it to start the osmosis of water and salting of the vegetable. With the correct percentage of salt in an anaerobic environment, the cabbage then starts to ferment as *Lactobacillus* grow and develop a distinctive sour flavour. Cabbage sauerkraut is the most iconic example of fermentation, practised in various forms for hundreds of years. It's now so well known across the globe that in many ways the word kraut has become synonymous with a way to describe a broader style of fermentation. I often make kraut from carrots, beetroot or a variety of cabbages using the same basic principles, and shredding or grating the veg for a greater surface area.

Makes a 1 litre/1¾ pint jar

1 whole white cabbage

3 per cent weight fine sea salt flakes
 (see method)

Pinch of caraway seeds, or to taste

Finely slice the cabbage by hand or try using (with care) a Japanese mandolin if you have one, until you have a large bowl of shredded cabbage. You can also try grating the core so you don't end up wasting any of it. Next, weigh the total quantity of cabbage in grams, then you need to calculate 3 per cent of this total weight to work out how much salt you will need (the calculation for this is to take the total weight of shredded cabbage, divide it by 100 and multiple by 3 to get the amount of salt in grams that you'll need). Weigh out that quantity of salt.

Sprinkle the cabbage evenly with the salt and the caraway seeds and firmly rub it in with your hands to break down the layers of cellulose and encourage the process of osmosis to start.

Cover the bowl with a damp cloth once you have released some briny water through massaging the cabbage and leave overnight at room temperature.

The next day, using a pestle or rolling pin, push the salted cabbage into a sterilised 1 litre/1¾ pint jar, making sure that no air pockets remain and that the cabbage is completely submerged in its own brine. This provides an anaerobic environment that will allow fermentation but prevent unwanted bacteria from thriving. Press the salted cabbage down beneath the surface of brine using a fermentation weight or a larger cabbage leaf folded in half.

Put the jar lid on, but leave it loose enough to allow the carbon dioxide to escape while the sauerkraut ferments. If you choose to tighten the lid on the jar fully at this stage, then you will need to release any carbon dioxide daily as it bubbles up in the jar. This is called burping (do this by gently unscrewing the lid, releasing any gases, then screwing the lid back on as before).

Leave to ferment at room temperature (18–22°C/64–72°F – warmer if you want a fast ferment, cooler if you want a slower, more full-bodied ferment) for 7–10 days. During this time, top up the ferment jar with a little water, if required, to keep the cabbage submerged under brine rather than exposed to open air.

Seal the jar tightly and store in the larder for up to 12 months. Once opened, keep refrigerated and use within 1–2 weeks. When serving, drain off the brine and try serving the sauerkraut on a cheeseboard, with cured meats or added to sandwiches for a delicious sour tangy flavour.

(Above) The essentials for kraut making.

(Above) A Japanese mandolin is a superb piece of kitchen kit to own for making kraut regularly at home but remember to be careful.

Salt Geek

Turmeric salt can be messy to make but is worth the effort and provides a splash of spicy colour to a dish with just a pinch. To make, grate 1–2 teaspoons of (peeled) fresh turmeric root into a bowl (wear kitchen/disposable gloves to avoid staining your hands) and mix with salt crystals, adding 1 tablespoon of salt at a time to the turmeric, until you have a beautiful golden sunset-orange salt. Add a few drops of water to help release the spice pigment onto the salt, then dry (spread out on a baking tray) in a very low oven at 75°C fan/203°F/gas oven as low as possible for about 1 hour, before cooling and storing in an airtight jar at room temperature for 6–12 months.

Golden Kraut

Some recipes are so easy that it's almost embarrassing to share them. This is one of my pantry secret weapons...a quick, easy recipe that's both colourful and delicious. This type of kraut is a twist on a classic cabbage sauerkraut but is just as sour and tangy in its own right. In fact, I'd go so far as to say that I may even prefer my golden kraut to the iconic cabbage version. It adds something extra special to some of my favourite ingredients and seems greater than the sum of its parts.

You can try the same technique with beetroot, sweet potato or any of your favourite root vegetables or tubers. I use root veg because I love the robust texture and earthy taste that works so well with sour pickled flavours, and texturally, root veg maintains a pleasant crunch after fermentation, which makes it versatile in the kitchen. The combo of spice and the sweet tang of grated fresh turmeric root with lots of crowd-pleasing carrot makes this ferment a magnificent addition to salads, burgers, tacos or a smoothie.

Makes a 500g/1lb 2oz jar

6 carrots, peeled and grated
(about 400g/14oz in total)
1 tbsp (peeled) grated fresh
turmeric root
1 tsp cumin seeds
3 per cent weight fine sea salt flakes
(see Sauerkraut recipe on page 124)

Place the carrots, turmeric and cumin seeds in a large bowl, mix well and then weigh the total amount. Next, calculate 3 per cent of this total weight to work out how much salt you need (see the Sauerkraut recipe on page 124 for how to calculate this). Weigh out this salt and then use your hands to massage the salt into the carrot mix for 2–3 minutes. I recommend wearing kitchen/disposable gloves to do this as the turmeric will stain your hands.

Cover the bowl with a damp tea towel and leave at a room temperature for 12–24 hours to kickstart fermentation. Transfer to a sterilised 500g/1lb 2oz jar. If you need to, top up the jar with a little water so that the level of the brine sits above the carrot.

Weigh it down with a fermentation weight or fill a small sandwich bag with water, seal and place on top of the carrot to keep it submerged under the brine. Put the jar lid on, but leave it loose enough to allow the carbon dioxide to escape while the kraut ferments.

Leave to ferment at room temperature (18–22°C/64–72°F – warmer if you want a fast ferment, cooler if you want a slower, more full-bodied ferment) for 7–10 days. Top up the jar with a little water during this time to keep the carrot mix submerged if some of the brine evaporates.

Seal the jar tightly and store in the larder for up to 12 months. Once opened, keep in the fridge and use within 2–3 weeks.

Try serving this kraut drained off with jacket potatoes, in a burrito or on the side of a vegetable curry.

Dill Cucumber Pickles

A timeless piece of salt craft that provides a shortcut to intense flavour in a recipe like a Haiku. To me, the juicy crunch, sour lactic tang, gentle anise, chilli heat and garlic is poetry. The bay leaves help provide extra flavour but also keep the cucumber texture crunchier.

Makes a 1 litre/1¾ pint jar

2 cucumbers, crinkle cut

2 garlic cloves, peeled

4 bay leaves

1 tsp chopped dill

1 tsp yellow mustard seeds

1 tsp black peppercorns

½ tsp dried chilli flakes

3 per cent weight fine sea salt flakes
   (see Sauerkraut recipe on page 124)

Mix all the ingredients (except the salt) in a large bowl, weigh, then calculate 3 per cent salt from this total weight (see the Sauerkraut recipe on page 124 for how to calculate this). Weigh out that salt. Dissolve this salt in 2 tablespoons of water to form a concentrated brine.

Pack the cucumber mix into a sterilised 1 litre/1¾ pint jar and then pour in the concentrated brine so the cucumber mix is fully submerged. Top up with a little water, if required.

Weigh it down with a fermentation weight or a clean stone. Put the jar lid on, but leave it loose enough to allow the carbon dioxide to escape while the pickles ferment.

Leave to ferment at room temperature (18–22°C/64–72°F – warmer if you want a fast ferment, cooler if you want a slower, more full-bodied ferment) for 7–10 days.

Seal the jar tightly and store in the fridge for up to 2–3 months. Once opened, consume within 1–2 weeks.

Try serving the pickles in burgers, with mayonnaise mixed into a tartare sauce or fried in a light beer batter as a snack with some hot pepper sauce.

Fermented Garlic Chutney

Hot garlic pickle is one of my favourite condiments with a curry or in a grilled cheese sandwich. For my version of a garlic chutney, I've taken the time to ferment the garlic, chilli and some limes for 7–10 days in advance. It's a hybrid between lime pickle and a fermented garlic preserve, with the fermented chilli and spices binding the flavours together as the glue, sweetened to soften the heat and finished by cooking slowly for an hour or two. The sour lactic tang is such an incredible way to emphasise the allium notes of the garlic while dampening its astringent notes. It mellows the longer you ferment it and can be a fantastic way to add an explosion of well-developed background flavour to a basic curry sauce.

Makes a 1 litre/1¾ pint jar

For the garlic ferment

6 bulbs garlic, cloves separated
   and peeled

2 limes, each sliced into eighths

2 red chillies, de-seeded and sliced

1 tsp fenugreek seeds

1 tsp nigella seeds

1 tsp coriander seeds

3 per cent weight *fleur de sel*
   (see Sauerkraut recipe on page 124)

For the chutney

1 x 400g/14oz tin chopped tomatoes

250g/9oz light soft brown sugar

150ml/¼ pint white wine vinegar

For the garlic ferment, mix the garlic, limes, chillies and spices in a bowl, then weigh the total amount. Calculate 3 per cent salt from this total weight (see the Sauerkraut recipe on page 124 for how to calculate this). Weigh out that amount of salt and dissolve in 2 tablespoons of water to form a concentrated brine.

Place the garlic mix into a sterilised 1 litre/1¾ pint jar. Pour in the concentrated brine, ensuring that the garlic is submerged and the ferment all sits under the brine level by adding a small fermentation weight or clean stone on top. Put the jar lid on, but leave it loose enough to allow the carbon dioxide to escape while the garlic mix ferments.

Leave to ferment at room temperature (18–22°C/64–72°F – warmer if you want a fast ferment, cooler if you want a slower, more full-bodied ferment) for 7–10 days.

Drain off and discard the brine once the garlic has fermented and the bubbling has ceased, then blitz all the ferment ingredients in a food processor to form a coarse chutney texture.

For the chutney, transfer the garlic chutney mix to a saucepan, add the tomatoes, sugar and vinegar and mix well with a wooden spoon.

Cook over a medium-low heat for 1–2 hours, stirring occasionally. Once the chutney is sticky and thick, it is ready to decant into a sterilised 1 litre/1¾ pint jar. Seal the jar and leave to cool. Store, unopened, in the larder for up to 12 months. Wait at least 48 hours before eating for best results, so the flavours can develop. Once opened, store in the fridge and use within 3–4 weeks.

This chutney is delicious spooned into curry sauces, layered in a cheese toastie or served with turmeric-roasted cauliflower.

Green Kimchi

This recipe is super-flexible and you can adapt the ingredients from season to season or depending on what you have in your garden. It's a great way to preserve leftovers and give them a fresh lease of life. My key advice is don't be shy with the chilli and ginger that you add to the mix as they really bring the ferment together, adding a strong kimchi vibe.

Makes a 1 litre/1¾ pint jar

Large handful of curly kale,
   roughly chopped
2 heads of spring greens or pointed
   cabbage, sliced
2 pak choi, sliced
2 spring onions, sliced
2 red chillies, de-seeded and sliced
1 tbsp (peeled) root ginger batons
3 per cent weight fine sea salt flakes
   (see Sauerkraut recipe on page 124)

Mix all the greens, chillies and ginger in a bowl, weigh, then calculate 3 per cent from this total weight (see the Sauerkraut recipe on page 124 for how to calculate this) and weigh out that amount of salt.

Mix the salt in with the greens mixture and start using your hands to massage the leaves and rub the salt into the veg. Really squeeze to break the cellulose layers and allow the salt to start its process of drawing out the moisture.

As you work the bowl for a few minutes, you will notice it starting to become wetter. At this point, transfer the mix into a sterilised 1 litre/ 1¾ pint jar and use your fist, a pestle or rolling pin to squeeze down the kimchi into the base of the jar so that you don't have any air bubbles left. Keep going until the greens are submerged under a layer of brine. Use a fermentation weight or a clean stone to keep the kimchi under the brine and out of air contact, but leave room for more brine to be drawn out of the vegetables as they ferment.

Put the jar lid on, but leave it loose enough to allow the carbon dioxide to escape while the kimchi ferments.

Leave to ferment at room temperature (18–22°C/64–72°F – warmer if you want a fast ferment, cooler if you want a slower, more full-bodied ferment) for 5–7 days.

Once it's ready, you can enjoy the kimchi straight away, or screw the lid on tightly and it will keep, unopened, in the larder for up to 12 months. Once opened, store in the fridge and use within 1–2 weeks.

This green kimchi is delicious added to a stir-fry just before serving, served with toasted muffins and devilled hollandaise sauce for a twist on eggs Florentine or with grilled halloumi and flatbread.

I think that fermented powders are going to erupt in the spice aisle and foodie scene within the next few years. When the green kimchi has fully fermented, you may also want to try dehydrating some of it to make a fermented seasoning powder. To do this, dry off the excess brine from the chopped kimchi on some kitchen paper or a tea towel. Lay out the kimchi in thin layers in a dehydrator. Leave to dry at 45–55°C/113–131°F for 10–12 hours until it's so dry that you can rub it into a powder. Using a spice grinder, blitz into a fine powder and store in a sealed jar in a cool, dry place for up to 12 months. You can also choose to add a little salt to taste prior to storing, but you will find it is already full of an umami-sour tang with a gorgeous salty edge. Sprinkle over salads, to season tofu or to finish scrambled eggs.

Fiery Kimchi

Make kimchi not war! This pungent, spicy ferment is one of my favourite things to eat in the entire world. It's great in a grilled cheese sandwich, on the side of a ploughman's or served in a big bowl of chicken noodle soup. I also highly recommend serving kimchi at breakfast with fried eggs or in a classic bacon butty for a tasty twist.

Makes a 1 litre/1¾ pint jar

2 heads Chinese leaf cabbage,
  shredded
2 carrots, peeled and grated
4 spring onions, finely sliced
4 garlic cloves, crushed
1 tbsp finely grated (peeled)
  root ginger
1 tsp dried chilli flakes
3 per cent weight fine sea salt flakes
  (see Sauerkraut recipe on page 124)

Make the kimchi at least a week in advance. Mix all the prepped vegetables, garlic and spices together in a bowl and weigh, then calculate 3 per cent from this total weight (see the Sauerkraut recipe on page 124 for how to calculate this). Weigh out that amount of salt. Sprinkle the salt over the kimchi veg mix and massage with your hands to work it into the cabbage and carrot. Cover with a damp tea towel and leave in the bowl at room temperature overnight.

The next day, push the kimchi down into a sterilised 1 litre/1¾ pint jar, adding the brine, too, then add enough water to make sure that the kimchi is covered with brine. Exclude all the air by tightly pressing down and covering the top of the kimchi with a fermentation weight or a clean stone.

Put the jar lid on, but leave it loose enough to allow the carbon dioxide to escape while the kimchi ferments.

Leave to ferment at room temperature (18–22°C/64–72°F – warmer if you want a fast ferment, cooler if you want a slower, more full-bodied ferment) for 7–10 days.

Once it's ready, you can enjoy the kimchi straight away, or screw the lid on tightly and it will keep, unopened, in the larder for up to 12 months. Once opened, store in the fridge and use within 2–3 weeks.

Kimchi Fried Rice

Kimchi tastes particularly fantastic with fried rice – just make sure you add it right at the end of cooking for a sweet and sour, spicy seasoning to the dish.

Serves 2

150g/5½oz wild rice

1 tbsp sesame oil

6 radishes, finely sliced

1 pak choi, sliced

4 tbsp Fiery Kimchi (see opposite)

2 tbsp toasted seeds (a mix of
   pumpkin and sunflower seeds fried
   with 1 tsp tamari sauce until lightly
   toasted)

1 tbsp finely chopped coriander

1 lime, sliced into quarters

First cook the rice according to the packet instructions, then drain.

Heat the sesame oil in a wok over a high heat, add the cooked rice, the radishes and pak choi and toss for 2–3 minutes, then add the kimchi. Stir-fry for 1–2 minutes to brown the veg slightly and take on the spicy kimchi flavours.

Serve sprinkled with the toasted seeds, chopped coriander and lime wedges on the side.

Fermented Chilli Sauce

The planet has gone a little bit sriracha crazy over the last few years and I can completely understand why. I make my own version with a base of fermented chilli. On its own, fermented chilli is divine. The Scoville heat softens a little when fermented but retains huge amounts of the chilli pepper's inherent flavour. My fermented chilli sauce is sweet and sour enough to spoon onto scrambled eggs, mix into pasta sauces or add to a taco as a fiery topping.

Comparing a bottle of homemade sriracha to the shop-bought versions is like comparing apples and pears but for me, the fermented chilli takes it to another level – I cannot emphasise strongly enough how amazingly tasty it is – welcome to the hot sauce revolution!

Makes about 750ml/26fl oz

For the fermented chilli

500g/1lb 2oz red chillies, de-seeded
   and stalks removed

15g/½oz fine sea salt flakes

For the sriracha sauce

1 x quantity Fermented Chilli
   (see above)

4 tbsp rice wine vinegar

4 tbsp garlic purée

2 tbsp finely grated (peeled)
   root ginger

2 tbsp fish sauce (optional)

85g/3oz light soft brown sugar

2 tsp runny honey

Sea salt and cracked black pepper

Ferment the chillies by blitzing them in a food processor with the salt to form a coarse chopped texture. Decant into a sterilised 500ml/18fl oz jar, cover with the lid and leave to ferment at room temperature (between 18–22°C/64–72°F) for 7–10 days. Release the build-up of gas daily by burping the jar. This involves opening the jar daily to allow carbon dioxide to escape and then resealing the jar. Alternatively, you can use a valved lid to ferment liquids and vegetable purées. Valved lids allow carbon dixoide to escape from the jar but don't allow air in – these one-way valves are particularly useful for liquid ferments which are more challenging to seal with a fermentation weight like you do with kraut or kimchi.

For the sriracha sauce, combine all the ingredients in a saucepan and bring gently to a simmer. Blitz until very smooth with a stick blender and then cook gently for a few minutes. Season to taste with salt and pepper, then transfer to a sterilised 750ml/26fl oz sauce bottle, seal, cool and store in the fridge. Unopened, this sauce will keep in the fridge for up to 2–3 months; once opened, use within 3–4 weeks.

Try using the sauce in a classic Marie rose sauce with prawns instead of tomato ketchup, or drizzle it over fried eggs and oyster mushrooms for a tangy brunch dish.

Fermented Potato Tacos

I fell in love with tacos when I worked my way through university as a chef in a Mexican restaurant. If I had a choice, I'd happily extend #TacoTuesday to the entire week. For this recipe, I've salted the potatoes and fermented them for three days to develop flavour. You can ferment them for longer but the aroma from fermented potato is strong and, from experience, I've found that a shorter ferment time is advisable.

For the filling, I've used some feta cheese and garlic-fried shiitake mushrooms with fermented carrot and roasted beetroot. The tacos are so delicious on their own, you could serve them simply with some salsa or guac.

Serves 2 (tacos)

For the fermented potato
1kg/2lb 4oz cold boiled potatoes
30g/1oz Dorset sea salt

For the tacos
200g/7oz Fermented Potato
200g/7oz plain flour, plus extra
1–2 tbsp natural yogurt (optional)
Vegetable oil, for greasing

For the garlic-fried mushrooms
100g/3½oz shiitake mushrooms, roughly chopped (leave small ones whole)
2 garlic cloves, sliced
½ tsp smoked paprika
½ tsp dried oregano
1 tbsp truffle oil
Sea salt and cracked black pepper

To finish and serve
1 lime, halved
Few pinches of pea shoots
Handful of fermented carrot (see Golden Kraut recipe on page 129)
115g/4oz roast beetroot, chopped (optional)
70g/2½oz marinated feta cheese, diced

For the fermented potato, mash the potato and weigh out the salt so that it is 3 per cent of the total weight of the potato (see the Sauerkraut recipe on page 124 for how to calculate this, but the weights given opposite should be about right). Mix the mashed potato and salt together, then place into a freezer bag and squeeze out the air. Leave to ferment at room temperature (between 18–22°C/64–72°F) for 3 days. Store leftover fermented potato in a sealed bag in the fridge (it will keep for up to 1 week) and try using it to make potato bread, fish cakes or add it to mashed potato.

For the tacos, combine the measured fermented potato with the flour in a bowl and knead into a dough. Add some yogurt if the mix is too dry, feels crumbly and won't bind together, or try some extra flour if the mashed fermented potato makes the dough on the wet side.

Divide the dough into 6–8 small balls, place on a tray and leave to rest in the fridge for 30 minutes.

On a lightly floured surface, roll out the balls of dough until they are nice and thin, approx. 10–15cm/4–6in in diameter, or use a tortilla press to flatten the dough into tacos.

Cook the tacos in batches on a preheated, oiled griddle over a medium-high heat for 2–3 minutes on each side until the tacos are cooked, pliable and no longer feel doughy, then keep them under a tea towel so they stay warm and pliable.

For the garlic-fried mushrooms, cook the mushrooms with the garlic, paprika, oregano and truffle oil in a frying pan over a medium heat for 4–5 minutes until golden brown, then season with salt and pepper.

To finish and serve, char the two lime halves, cut-side down, on the hot griddle to blacken and caramelise – this will bring out some extra sweetness to squeeze over the top of the tacos when you serve. Layer each taco with a pinch of pea shoots, some fermented carrot, roast beetroot, feta cheese and herb oil, then serve each portion with a charred lime half for squeezing over.

Chapter Twelve
Salt Blocks

When I worked in a Mexican restaurant, the showstopper from the kitchen was the sizzling steak fajita special. A cast-iron skillet plate heated to volcanic temperatures in the oven was then served with strips of 48-hour marinated beef dropped onto the hot metal with tongs. Fat and flavour evaporated in an instant hissing sizzle, a bellowing spiced steam-cloud following behind the waiter like the puff from a steam engine. An intoxicating combination of charred browning meat and spices filling the sombrero-clad ceiling and converting a few more customers to the Specials menu.

It was memorable to me because the theatre of food is always worth exploring and embracing, and I've used salt blocks now for many years. Many people have probably bought them with the intention of using them, then they only appear once in a pink moon, but I believe that salt blocks are both functional and attention-grabbing for all the right reasons. I hope to equip you with a few more ideas that will encourage you to use them more often.

What are Salt Blocks?

Salt blocks are mined from Himalayan rock salt as large, meteor-like boulders and are later carved or sliced into slabs, blocks, bricks and bowls. Almost all the salt blocks you will find come from Pakistan. The Khewra mine is the largest in the area and produces billions of tons of salt every year. They still use an old 'room and pillar' method, whereby roughly 50 per cent of the salt is left to support the ceilings. The Khewra mine is surrounded by other thriving smaller mines such as Kalabagh, Karak and Jatta. Mining is environmentally questionable, but I appreciate that buying salt blocks supports local economies which are trying to do more and more to safeguard the welfare of their employees. There are obviously some very contentious sustainability issues around mining but, in terms of salt resources, there is an enormous amount, so it won't run out for millennia. Look to buy salt blocks that are at least 2.5cm/1in thick and avoid opaque, milky-coloured blocks; instead choose ones with a densely packed pink hue.

How to Use

I use salt blocks to bake with, barbecue and grill, but I also use them chilled for light cures and serving unseasoned raw shellfish on as an impressive platter. If you are cooking on them, it's vital to manage the rate of heating them up. If they are heated or chilled too quickly, they can crack as any moisture trapped in them expands. The slower you heat a block, the longer it lasts.

Salt blocks take a long time to heat up and while they can store extreme warmth to radiate back onto food, they do not like to be heated or cooled quickly. Use them like a pizza stone or cast-iron skillet. Try preheating the salt block in an oven (place it in the cold oven when you turn it on) at 160°C fan/350°F/gas mark 4 for 30 minutes, then remove it from the oven for 15 minutes. Increase the temperature to 200°C fan/425°F/gas mark 7, then return the salt block to the oven and heat for another 30 minutes. If you heat or chill the block too quickly, it can crack.

(Above) Tuna steak

How Do They Work?

Salt blocks used properly will provide those addictive salty, toasty flavours. They are carved so that food can be cooked directly on top of them, like a pizza stone or heavy-duty cast-iron skillet. They can also be used to dry-age, cure or serve food on. Moist foods pick up the salty flavour much more than dry and I cure thinly sliced meats, like a beef carpaccio, or fish/shellfish, like tuna and scallops, on them in the fridge. You can observe the curing process happening before your eyes and it's a really effective tool.

When heated, the intense heat of the salt block both sears and browns proteins at the same time as it caramelises sugars. If preheated slowly to a high temperature, you can achieve a crisp cooked surface with a thin layer of salt glazing the browned crust. The only real danger is when moisture from the food dissolves on the block or the block is not hot enough. This way you risk ending up with a pool of salty liquid that over-seasons the food. Make sure the salt block is always hot enough to sizzle off a few drops of moisture and sear rather than slow cook the food, which will result in a briny pool leaching onto the block.

Cleaning and Storage

Don't clean a salt block when it's very hot. Allow to cool first and then use a stiff washing-up brush and some hot water, but don't use soap or you can taint the flavour of the block. The same applies to when cleaning a cold (unheated) salt block or a salt bowl. Salt blocks are naturally anti-fungal and anti-microbial, but if you want to freshen them, rub with a slice of lemon.

I have a collection of salt blocks and carved salt bowls hiding in cupboards, on top of shelves and under the stairs around my house. Due to the humid Cornish weather and being so close to the coast, my blocks need to be wrapped up to keep them dry. Salt is by its nature hygroscopic or moisture-attracting, so try to keep humidity to a minimum. Store them in a dry sunny spot like a windowsill or wrapped in a towel and in a sealed plastic bag or container.

(Right) Dry ageing over chunks of pink rock salt allows great air circulation around steaks.

Dry Aged Steak

For me, there's a palatable difference when steak is dry-aged compared to wet steak. As it ages, the beef develops a nutty, earthy flavour. It tastes beefier when it's cooked, more like rare roast beef, with an almost game-like complexity. The process is relatively simple and is a great way to enhance a good-quality piece of meat simply by using salt to create a richer taste.

Serves 2

1 x 500g/1lb 2oz prime côte de boeuf
   (ribeye) steak
1 Himalayan salt block, about
   30 x 20 x 4cm/12 x 8 x 1½in
A little rock salt, grated (optional)
Splash of olive oil
Sea salt and cracked black pepper

For the herby garlic butter
25g/1oz unsalted butter, softened
1 garlic clove, crushed
2 sprigs thyme or rosemary, leaves
   picked and roughly chopped
Pinch of sea salt flakes, plus extra
   to finish
Pinch of cracked black pepper

Place the steak on a wire rack above the salt block. At this point, you can also dust it with an extremely fine layer of grated rock salt, if you like. Place into the fridge. Try to only use enough salt at this stage to season the steak lightly and allow for a gentle osmosis on the surface, but not so much as to draw out all the moisture like a dry cure.

If room allows, put the salt block, rack and steak in a sealed container in the fridge, but this may not be possible due to space – I find the salad box section in my fridge is perfect, or place into a large plastic container with a lid.

Turn the steak every couple of days and wipe up any moisture from the block.

Leave to dry age for a minimum of 10 days. After 14–28 days, the steak starts developing nutty, beefy flavours. After 30–45 days, the beef gets pretty funky. This is still okay to eat but it's an acquired taste – the result of enzymes changing and tenderising the beef.

To cook, remove the steak from the fridge 30–60 minutes before you plan to cook it. Make a herby garlic butter by combining the butter, garlic, herbs, salt and pepper in a small bowl. Season the steak and rub it with a little olive oil.

Cook the steak in a preheated hot frying pan or griddle over a hot fire or stove for about 15 minutes for medium-rare, basting it with the herby garlic butter as you go, until the steak is firmer to the touch and nicely caramelised and browned on the surface. Transfer the steak to a plate, cover with foil and allow to rest for 5–6 minutes, then drizzle over the buttery cooking juices and serve. Finish with a few salt flakes at the table for extra crunch.

You can also dry age other ingredients such as duck breast, venison and other beef cuts by draping them over a simple bed of large rock salt crystals – rough-cut lumps placed in a tray like boulders on the beach. The key is to allow room for air to circulate and to turn the food every so often. Airflow is important when dry ageing so that you don't end up with moisture pooling on the surface of the aged ingredient. Pooling of brine can build a bridge for osmosis to cure it too quickly and, through diffusion, risk too much salt making its way deep into the cells of the food. If you have a meat fridge, keeping a collection of salt crystals inside it is a good way to enhance the flavour of prime cuts.

Dry ageing fish is also becoming more common now among chefs and is regularly found on good seafood menus. Fundamentally, dry aged fish follows the same principles as meat. Drawing out moisture ages the fish and intensifies the natural flavours while it is still fresh. When it is then cooked, it'll be extra juicy as it absorbs flavours from stocks or sauces more quickly. The fish can be aged above salt blocks in the same way as beef, or it can be aged in its own stand-alone fridge hanging from (butcher's) hooks with salt blocks installed to help slowly draw out moisture from the air. My hope one day is to have a small refrigerated larder clad in salt block tiles on the walls for dry ageing all my ingredients – I think that my chances are very slim but you can always dream.

Scallop Ceviche

Good-quality fresh shellfish/seafood from clean waters can be eaten raw, but you can add more flavour when it is lightly cured, plus the process tightens up the texture to provide a little more bite. Razor-thin slithers of sliced scallop on a salt block will cure in minutes and the lime segments to accompany make this a wonderfully quick ceviche to make at home. I also love to add diced cucumber, chilli rings and dill to enhance the clean taste of the sea. Try serving this with a classic Margarita or some tequila slammers for a zingy way to kickstart a party.

Serves 2

4 fresh scallops, shucked

1 Himalayan salt block, about
    30 x 20 x 2.5cm/12 x 8 x 1in

½ red chilli, thinly sliced

1 tbsp diced cucumber

Grated zest and segmented flesh of
    1 lime (keep the segmented halves
    for juice)

Dill or fennel fronds, to finish

Clean the scallop shells and remove and discard the corals. Wash the scallops under cold running water to remove any sand or grit and pat dry with kitchen paper. Thinly slice the scallops across the flesh.

Gently place the scallop slices onto the salt block and leave to cure at room temperature for 5–10 minutes. Add the chilli slices, diced cucumber and lime segments to the block after curing to garnish the dish and provide fresh bursts of flavour. Finish with the lime zest and fresh dill or fennel fronds.

Serve straight from the salt block at the table or return the ceviche to the cleaned shells, and drizzle with the juice leftover from segmenting the lime.

Venison Tartare

Wild food can liberate you from the usual kitchen rules. It inspires a certain creative freedom with cooking methods and demands seasonality on its own terms. To me, preparing a tartare is a process that's almost rhythmic – finely dicing shallot, cornichons and capers, then the repetitive knife work that it takes to prepare a lean cut of steak, a fillet of wild salmon or a venison loin and cleanly transform it into a sharp-edged mince that mirrors the size of your finely diced flavourings. It's a mixing desk of flavours with a metallic salted tang, briny waves and mustard heat. Eating lightly cured meat is special. There is a raw, clean purity to the dish, which I find captivating. I love a lightly cured quail's egg headlining this ensemble and black garlic playing a balsamic sweet, umami beat backing up the band.

Serves 2

For the tartare

400g/14oz venison steak
  (choose lean, best-quality meat)
1 Himalayan salt block, about
  20 x 10 x 2.5cm/8 x 4 x 1in
½ shallot, finely diced
4–6 cornichons, finely diced
1 tsp capers in brine or vinegar,
  drained and finely chopped
1 black garlic clove, finely diced
1 tsp finely chopped chives
1 tsp tarragon Dijon mustard
1 tsp truffle oil
½ tsp sherry vinegar
Pinch of cracked black pepper
Pinch of Beetroot Salt (see below)

For the beetroot salt

½ raw beetroot, peeled and grated
125g/4½oz sea salt flakes

To serve

2 quail's egg yolks, plus 2 spare egg
  yolks (in case of breakages when plating)
1 tsp Beetroot Salt (see above)
2 handfuls of rocket leaves

First, make the beetroot salt by blitzing the grated beetroot and salt flakes together in a food processor until bright pink. You only need a little for this recipe, so store the leftover beetroot salt in a sealed sterilised jar in a cool, dark cupboard for up to 3 months. It can be kept and used long after this point safely, but the colour can fade and the flavour diminishes.

To cure the quail's egg yolks (to serve), place the four egg yolks in a small bowl, cover with a light sprinkle of the measured beetroot salt and leave to cure at room temperature for 1 hour. This makes them easier to handle and place on the dish later, it seasons them perfectly and adds a subtle earthy, sweet note to complement the venison.

Meanwhile, for the tartare, slice the venison across the grain into thin slices and then, using a sharp chef's knife, cut each slice into small cubes. Try to work as neatly and precisely as possible when preparing the meat so that it doesn't turn mushy later. Once you have diced all the venison, chop it further for a uniform dice so that you have a texture that resembles a coarse mince (similar in size to the diced shallot, etc). Spread this meat out on the salt block and leave to cure at room temperature for 20–30 minutes.

Remove the venison from the salt block and pat dry with kitchen paper to remove any moisture drawn out while curing.

Whisk together the shallot, cornichons, capers, black garlic, chives, mustard, truffle oil and vinegar in a small bowl to make a dressing. Toss this dressing with the cured venison mince. The salt block semi-curing process helps the venison absorb all the other aromatic flavours from the tartare and soak in the dressing for extra oomph.

Season the tartare to taste with a pinch each of black pepper and beetroot salt – you won't need much at all, so taste a spoonful first. Alexanders seeds also work well for a foraged alternative to black pepper in this dish.

Just before serving, wash the cured quail's egg yolks under cold gently running water to remove the salt before serving and pat dry with kitchen paper. (Any spare cured egg yolks can be kept in their cure in an airtight container in the fridge and used within 1 week. Use to garnish salads.)

For each serving, using a baking ring, spoon the venison tartare onto a handful of rocket leaves on each plate and top with a cured quail's egg yolk.

Salt-pressed Cucumbers

This method would also work well with thin slices of aubergine, courgette or tomato. The heavy salt blocks simultaneously compress the cucumber slices and season them. After salting you can submerge the pressed cucumbers in water, as the salty cucumbers make a light brine in the water that's also ideal to ferment. This is a rustic way to draw out moisture, amplify flavour and preserve vegetables.

Try pressing all sorts of fruit and veg this season. The combination of bay, dill, mustard, chilli and garlic with cucumber is a classic. However, if you want something more radical, try salting pears sprinkled with soft brown sugar, then after pressing, soak them in bourbon. Press fennel bulbs after they've been passed through a mandolin and pickle to serve with fish or in a zingy remoulade. Press heritage tomatoes and then blitz with stale bread for an intense summer gazpacho.

Makes 600g/1lb 5oz

2 cucumbers, sliced in half lengthways

2 Himalayan salt blocks, each about
  20 x 15 x 5cm/8 x 6 x 2in

1 tbsp chopped dill

½ tsp yellow mustard seeds

½ tsp dried chilli flakes

2 garlic cloves, sliced

4 bay leaves

Start by slicing the cucumber halves lengthways into uniform strips and then place them onto the surface of one of the salt blocks. Sprinkle with the dill, mustard seeds and chilli flakes. Next, add the garlic and bay leaves to the gaps in between the cucumber strips.

Place the second salt block on top of the cucumber strips. Leave to press for 1 hour at room temperature and then turn the cucumber strips over. Repeat and leave to press between the salt blocks for another hour.

Serve the salt-pressed cucumber strips with burgers, or finely chopped in couscous, or submerge the salty cucumbers in water and leave to lacto-ferment in their own diffused brine until they turn into sour pickles after 7–10 days – do this in the same way you would make Sauerkraut and keep them submerged in a sterilised jar with a fermentation weight on top (see Sauerkraut recipe on pages 124-5 for more info on how to do this). If storing dry pressed cucumbers, then keep in an airtight container in the fridge for up to 10 days.

(Left) Aubergine seasoned with za'atar and sea salt flakes reduces the bitterness and removes some moisture. Sliced aubergine is superb pressed between two heavy salt blocks and then grilled over charcoal to caramelise and enhance the subtle sweet notes.

Salt-block Baked Salmon

Baking with a salt block is dead easy and delivers strong mineral seasoning directly onto your food as it cooks. My advice would be to avoid adding any further salt to this recipe and coat your fish and vegetables with a little oil before baking to protect them from becoming overly salty. A thick slab of salt provides an amazing level of conducted heat which radiates like a pizza stone when heated, but make sure you preheat it first to sear the fish. As a result, you will find that cooking times can be faster than normal, and your fish may be cooked in as little as 7–8 minutes. Don't be shy with freshly squeezed lemon juice to finish the asparagus, and a good hit of chilli in the devilled hollandaise helps to cut through this naturally salty salmon bake.

Serves 2

1 Himalayan salt block, about
  30 x 20 x 4cm/12 x 8 x 1½in
2 wild salmon fillets (skin-on), about
  400g/14oz total weight
1 tbsp olive oil
Pinch of cracked black pepper
8 vine tomatoes, left whole
  on the vine
Handful of asparagus spears,
  trimmed and left whole
Grated zest and juice of 1 lemon
1 tsp finely chopped parsley
1 tbsp chopped coriander, to garnish

For the devilled hollandaise
250g/9oz salted butter, diced
4 large free-range egg yolks
1 garlic clove, minced
½ tsp Dijon mustard
1 tsp lemon juice
1 tsp hot chilli sauce

Place the salt block into a cold oven and then heat the oven to 160°C fan/350°F/gas mark 4. Remove the salt block from the oven, then after 15 minutes, return it to the oven, increase the temperature to 200°C fan/425°F/gas mark 7 and heat for another 30 minutes.

Meanwhile, make the devilled hollandaise. Melt the butter in a bain-marie, then slowly whisk it into a separate large, heatproof bowl with the egg yolks and garlic. Beat until you have a smooth, velvety sauce, then add the mustard, lemon juice and hot chilli sauce. Return to the bain-marie and keep whisking for 2–3 minutes until the sauce thickens slightly. Remove from the heat, cover and keep somewhere warm while you bake the fish.

Coat the salmon in a little of the olive oil and season with a pinch of black pepper, then place the fillets onto the hot salt block, skin-side down. Dress the tomatoes and asparagus with a little drizzle of the remaining oil and some lemon juice. Sprinkle the lemon zest and parsley over the asparagus, then place on the salt block with the tomatoes, alongside the salmon, and bake for 7–8 minutes until the fish is cooked and the veg are soft and tender.

Remove from the oven and squeeze some more lemon juice over the asparagus. Pour the devilled hollandaise sauce over the salt-baked salmon, garnish with the coriander and serve the hot salt block at the table.

155

Salt-block Burgers

A burger can be at risk of drying out when it's suspended over the fierce heat of an exposed grill and the meat juices and moisture drain from the mince too quickly, leaving it dry or causing flare-ups as the fat hits the flames, creating a tainted charcoal flavour. This method of cooking removes that charred profile and instead leaves a clean, juicy, perfectly seasoned burger. The secret to success with these burgers is the salty crust that forms on the beef as it grills and a sweet, punchy, umami flavour where it cooks directly on the block and the beef caramelises and browns. The salt block seasons the patty while allowing it to remain super-succulent because the strong radiated heat from the hot salt block works simultaneously with the oven's convection heat.

One of my guilty pleasures is a slice of neon orange burger cheese on a quality homemade beef patty. It's an odd paradox pairing gourmet grass-fed beef with a sort of Homer Simpson junk food nostalgia – but it works for me!

Serves 4

1 Himalayan salt block, about
   40 x 20 x 4cm/16 x 8 x 1½in

For the burger patties
1 shallot, finely diced
1 tbsp vegetable oil, plus extra
   for drizzling
1kg/2lb 4oz minced beef
½ tsp grated nutmeg
½ tsp cracked black pepper
Small pinch of sea salt
4 slices cheese, such as Gouda,
   Emmental or burger cheese (optional)

To serve
4 brioche rolls
Salad leaves
Dill Cucumber Pickles (see page 130)
Ketchup or burger relish
Chips or a chopped salad

Place the salt block into a cold oven and then heat the oven to 160°C fan/350°F/gas mark 4 for 30 minutes. Remove the salt block from the oven, then after 15 minutes, return it to the oven, increase the temperature to 200°C fan/425°F/gas mark 7 and heat for another 30 minutes.

While the salt block preheats, make the burger patties. Caramelise the shallot in a small frying pan with the oil over a medium-low heat for about 15 minutes, then allow to cool to room temperature.

Mix the caramelised shallot with the minced beef and season with the nutmeg, pepper and salt, then form into four large patties by hand.

Drizzle the beef patties with a little oil, then place them onto the hot salt block and bake for 5–6 minutes. Flip the burgers and bake for a further 5–6 minutes until they've developed a good crust and the meat has caramelised. Add the slices of cheese (if using) and cook for a further 2–3 minutes so the cheese melts.

Meanwhile, split and lightly toast the brioche rolls and get the salad leaves, pickles, ketchup/relish and chips/chopped salad ready.

Build the burgers in the toasted rolls on a bed of salad leaves with the pickles and ketchup/relish. Serve with chips or a chopped salad.

Salt-bowl Tarragon Mayo

A salt bowl is a kind of ancient alchemist's cauldron that transforms the contents with a crystal shine and a gentle shifty smile as the shaped salt bowl dissolves in slow motion and, over time, curves deeper with each recipe it conjures up.

I don't think I will make mayonnaise in any other bowl ever again. As a chef, if there is a way that you can remove an ingredient from your shopping list but still achieve more flavour in a dish, then it's a no-brainer.

I confess to being more than slightly obsessed with tarragon mayo. To me, the addition of tarragon to a mustard, mayonnaise or hollandaise lifts the flavour with the perfect level of anise lightness, elevating the humble classics. I hope this recipe inspires you to treat yourself to a salt bowl and unleashes your inner salt magic – making fresh mayonnaise is something that is often overlooked by home cooks, but a plate of French fries has never tasted so good as when dipped in this pure velvet gold.

Makes 300g/10½oz

2 rich free-range egg yolks

1 Himalayan salt bowl, about
   15cm/6in diameter

1 tsp tarragon Dijon mustard

1 tbsp white wine vinegar

300ml/½ pint cold-pressed
   rapeseed oil

1 tbsp chopped tarragon, or to taste

1 tsp garlic purée, or to taste

Place the egg yolks into the salt bowl, then add the mustard and vinegar and whisk until you have a smooth paste.

Keep whisking continuously while gradually pouring in the oil in a slow, steady stream. The mayo will come together and thicken after about 3–4 minutes and then you can add the tarragon and garlic purée to taste.

Serve immediately or transfer the mayo to a sealed container and store in the fridge for up to 1 week.

Salt Geek

*A salt bowl is quite frankly a cool piece of kit to own – the possibilities are endless....
Try using it as a multifunctional mixing bowl – to make dressings, serve salads or to finish salted caramel. I love the simplicity of not needing to add salt to a recipe and instead relying on the mineral concave curves to brush the food with a clean layer of salt as the ingredients move over the pink surface.*

Chapter Thirteen
Salt Baking

Cracking open a salt crust is a kitchen moment that captures the imagination. Like dunking sourdough soldiers into a boiled egg, carving a slow-smoked brisket to reveal that tandoori-magenta smoke ring or cracking last year's foraged walnuts next to a crackling fire – immensely satisfying and elusive moments when all your senses combine. Salt baking delivers this every time.

The first time I ever salt baked food was on a nautical adventure for a TV series called *The Hungry Sailors* that was filmed ten years ago. The show involved sailing around the south coast of England with my dad, Dick Strawbridge, and gathering ingredients to cook up a storm on a wooden pilot cutter. We cooked a whole wild sea bass in a salt crust in the galley kitchen and cracked it open together on deck. The first time you attempt a new piece of salt craft is rarely perfect but, on this occasion, it was bang on – or as my dad says, I'd rather be lucky than smart. The fish was moist, flaky and clean with a seasoning that defied logic, almost as though it had been cooked by invisible brackish steam suffused from the salt crust. The rock-hard salt it was baked beneath forged into a crystalline mortar, wrapping the fish in a glistening seawall to protect it from the fierce oven swell.

Principles of Salt Baking

The principles of salt baking are simple and date back, on record, to around 400 BC. Essentially, it's about making a salty mixture that you wrap around your food before baking. It can range in consistency from a light whipped meringue to a sticky bread dough and the simplest version is just salt mixed with enough water to make a wet-sand mixture. The results are never disappointing – when you crack open the hard golden shell, you reveal the fragrant prize, soft and steaming beneath.

The protective layer of salt forms an insulating layer around the food that traps moisture inside – a bit like cooking in an *en papillote* parcel but more robust. The additional element is, of course, the seasoning. The outside of your food will be very salty as the salts dissolve on the surface and through osmosis they start to penetrate the food. This is why I usually only salt bake with larger ingredients that I can then peel/skin before serving.

The cooking time is also key – allow at least an extra 50 per cent cooking time compared to normal baking for the food to bake under the salt crust. Salt is a really poor conductor of heat, which is why it's such an effective insulation for the food buried beneath. Salt crusts are essentially an oven within an oven that insulates and cooks your food gently and evenly – the ultimate salty low and slow technique to master. The result is juicy, moist and nutritionally-rich food as the natural juices are locked in rather than evaporating. Less flavour is lost, too, and it is a sure-fire way to avoid drying out ingredients, hence, it's often used with whole fish.

The salt crust itself is inedible so don't be tempted to try and eat it. This is unfortunately what makes this method of cooking with salt expensive and wasteful. So let's address that issue…I don't like to use and then throw away huge amounts of salt as the whole process is extravagant, so I always reduce the salt percentage and bulk it out with flour or egg whites. When selecting which salt to use, I recommend using either rock salt, fine flakes or small crunchy crystals, but not table salt. Despite being cheap, table salt won't add much to a recipe in terms of flavour.

Adding Flavours

You can be as adventurous as your imagination allows with salt baking. Add any flavours to the salt dough to capture a theatrical sense of fun and incorporate layers of aroma that build anticipation of what's hidden below as you crack open the baked cocoon.

Mixing aromatic herbs and spices in with your salt for flavour makes a massive difference when salt baking. If you are salt baking a whole fish, make sure that you stuff the cavity with some lemongrass or fresh herbs, like when you roast a whole chicken in the oven. Stuffing the fish provides a layer of aromatics that will steam and bounce around within the salt shell dome like ocean sounds in a conch spiral. Or you could lay the food on a flat bed of sliced aromatics – try fennel, citrus or fresh herb stalks – then cover it all with the salt dough.

Salt dough is a creative chrysalis that hatches new ideas before your eyes. Liberate your inner salt geek and bring the whole tray to the table to crack open with your friends and family.

(Above) Fennel

Salt-baked Beetroot

Beetroot has a metallic earthy flavour that lends itself perfectly to salt baking. The fresh salty tang of the crust steams the beets and traps in their moisture while they bake. Once you crack open the salty dough and reveal the beetroot, it should be soft enough to cut with a spoon.

Serves 4

1kg/2lb 4oz sea salt crystals

4 tbsp plain flour

2 egg whites, beaten

1 tbsp chopped dill (optional)

8–12 raw beetroots, scrubbed
and unpeeled

Preheat the oven to 180°C fan/400°F/gas mark 6 and line a baking tray with baking parchment.

Measure 100ml/3½fl oz of water in a jug. In a large bowl, mix the salt with the flour, beaten egg whites and the measured water. Stir in the chopped dill (if using) and add a little more water if required, so that the salt dough reaches the consistency of wet sand.

Place the beetroot (close together) on the lined baking tray and then cover them with the salt-crust mixture so there is an even layer about 2–3cm/¾–1¼in thick. Try to avoid gaps in the crust.

Bake for 1½ hours until the salt crust is solid and if you run the back of a knife across it, it crinkles like crackling.

Allow to rest for 10–15 minutes, then crack open and either peel the beets or lightly brush off any excess salt before serving.

Salt-baked beetroot is fantastic thinly sliced with goats' cheese in a grilled sandwich, added to coleslaw with chopped dill and grated orange zest for a well-seasoned burst of earthy flavour, or mixed with tahini and cooked chickpeas for a bright pink hummus.

Salt-baked Wild Bass

I've salt-baked all sorts of fish and there is a tendency to see the salt-baking part as a form of showmanship that eclipses the seafood hidden beneath. You can bake a fish in a salt crust that's almost completely made with salt – sparkling, crystal-studded and rock hard. It works fantastically – much like the salt-baked beetroot – but as a chef, I've come to prefer a lighter salt crust with fish that's more akin to a savoury meringue.

This salt crust is easier to peel off in cracked chunks after cooking, without peppering the fish with salt as you break into the baked crust – which can risk over-seasoning the fish as you excavate it. For my bass, I have included some dill in the salt crust mix and set the fish on an aromatic bed of anise and citrus which suffuses into the fish as it steams under the lighter salt crust. There's nothing pretentious about this cooking method and I strongly recommend having a go and cracking the fear factor that swims around fish cookery. If done correctly, salt baking fish keeps it moist, flaky and seasoned with a soft sea breeze.

Serves 2

For the salt crust

6 egg whites

250g/9oz sea salt flakes (see Salt
   Choice, overleaf)

1 tbsp finely chopped dill

For the salt-baked bass

½ fennel bulb, thinly sliced

½ pink grapefruit, thinly sliced

1 whole wild sea bass (approx.
   800g/1lb 12oz), gutted and de-scaled

Bunch of tarragon

For the salad

½ fennel bulb, thinly sliced

½ cucumber, peeled and diced

2 tbsp sprouted seeds (selection of
   sprouted mung beans, chickpeas and/
   or sunflower seeds)

½ pink grapefruit, segmented

1 shallot, finely diced

1 tsp truffle oil

1 tsp white wine vinegar

Sea salt and cracked black pepper

Preheat the oven to 180°C fan/400°F/gas mark 6.

To make the salt crust, whisk the egg whites in a bowl until stiff, then, using a metal spoon or sharp spatula, fold in the salt and dill. Try to keep some air in the mixture.

For the sea bass, lay the fennel and grapefruit on a baking tray. Stuff the cavity of the bass with the tarragon, then lay the fish on top of the fennel and grapefruit. Gently spread the salty meringue mixture over the fish (including the fennel and grapefruit) to cover it completely.

Bake for 25–30 minutes until the salt crust is hard to the touch and pale golden in colour.

While the fish is baking, toss all the salad ingredients together in a large bowl, seasoning to taste with salt and pepper.

Remove the fish from the oven. Crack open the salt crust with the back of a heavy knife and then peel off the crust in chunks.

Serve the baked sea bass with the fresh, zingy salad.

Sicilian sea salt

Sicilian sea salt from Trapani is a great choice for this bass recipe. The salt is harvested from the north-west coast of Sicily and the moisture evaporates due to the summer sun and strong African winds. The *fiore di sale* are the young salt crystals that form on the top and are naturally rich in iodine, magnesium and potassium. These finer grains are excellent for a light salt crust and mix extremely well with the egg whites for a robust spreadable structure that locks in flavour and dissolves quickly over the fish to season.

Salt-crusted Lamb

The first time I baked lamb wrapped in a salt dough crust was one winter a few years ago in an underground oven on a bed of hot rocks. Back then, I flavoured the rustic wholemeal salt dough with chopped nettles and, after several hours of cooking, the lamb took on an earthy, metallic tang that blew my mind. I have been hooked on this method ever since.

The combination of wild thyme and roasted garlic salt in this spring version is mouth-wateringly tasty and the sacrificial wild garlic wrapped around the lamb adds a fresh allium perfume when you crack open the hardened crust to reveal the wonderfully moist meat within.

Serves 4

For the lamb
2 tbsp The Full Works Sauce
   (see page 120)
1 tbsp extra virgin olive oil
1 tbsp chopped thyme leaves
1 tbsp crushed garlic
1 tsp fennel seeds
1 tsp sea salt flakes
½ tsp cracked black pepper
1.5–2kg/3lb 5oz–4lb 8oz half leg
   of lamb (bone-in)
Large bunch of wild garlic leaves

For the salt dough
5 egg whites
700g/1lb 9oz plain flour, plus a little
   extra for rolling
400g/14oz roasted garlic salt
1 tbsp chopped thyme leaves

To serve
400g/14oz new potatoes
   (I used homegrown Apache
   potatoes), boiled
120g/4¼oz green beans, trimmed
   and steamed
200g/7oz frozen garden peas, boiled
55g/2oz salted butter, diced
1 tbsp chopped mint

For the lamb, in a small mixing bowl, combine The Full Works Sauce, the oil, thyme, garlic, fennel seeds, salt and pepper. Rub this mixture all over the lamb leg, then place in a dish, cover and leave to marinate in the fridge for at least 2 hours but ideally overnight.

Preheat the oven to 160°C fan/350°F/gas mark 4.

Now go to work on making the rustic salt dough. Beat the egg whites in a bowl until light and fluffy, then set to one side. In another bowl, combine the flour, garlic salt, thyme and 250ml/9fl oz of water. Gradually fold in the egg whites to form a wet consistency dough that is just firm enough to knead. If required, add more flour, and then using the extra, roll out on a board so the dough is big enough to enclose the lamb completely.

Wrap the marinated lamb in the wild garlic leaves and then place it in the centre of the salt dough. Fold the dough over and wrap the lamb like a parcel so it's completely covered, then place, seam-side down, on a roasting tray. Roast for 4½–5 hours until the salt dough crust is rock hard, dark brown and the lamb inside is cooked. Make a hole in the crust with a metal skewer and insert a meat thermometer probe to check the internal lamb temperature is between 60–70°C/140–158°F.

Allow to rest for 20–30 minutes, then crack open the crust to reveal the perfectly seasoned lamb inside. It should fall off the bone. Carve the lamb and serve with the boiled and steamed vegetables, topped with the butter and chopped mint.

Salt-baked Squash

Baking in straw or hay is perfect for salt baking larger vegetables, whole brined chickens or joints of meat. It's also a great way to make your salt go further when making a salt dough. When mixed, the combination of barley straw, sea salt and flour resembles a rustic building material like cob. The combination of salt and straw has got great thermal properties so food takes longer to cook, but it's worth the wait.

Serves 4

4 egg whites, beaten

250g/9oz sea salt

250g/9oz plain flour

Large handful of barley straw or
　　hay (enough to loosely cover your
　　squash and hide it in a nest, plus
　　extra for lining the baking tray)

1 large acorn squash (you could
　　also use butternut, red kuri or
　　Crown Prince)

Preheat the oven to 160°C fan/350°F/gas mark 4.

Make a rustic salt crust by folding the beaten egg whites with the salt and flour in a large bowl. Mix in the straw or hay, then add 150ml/ ¼ pint of water so that it's wet and sticky.

Lay a small handful of straw or hay over the bottom of a baking tray and then place the squash on top. Cover the squash completely with the straw and salt mixture, leaving no gaps.

Bake the squash for 4 hours until it's soft inside and the salt crust hardens and changes in colour to a dark brown – test with a skewer to see if the squash is tender and cooked.

Crack open the salt crust with a knife and break it apart. Cut off the top of the squash and scoop out the seeds. The skin is inedible but the flesh should be perfectly soft and ready to serve.

Try serving salt-baked squash with Puy lentils, pickled walnuts and rocket pesto, or blitzed into a soup with chestnuts and apple, or to bind together fishcakes with smoked haddock and cauliflower.

Straw and Salt Squash Gnocchi

Homemade gnocchi can be quite a handful to make at home, but in my opinion, it's worth every ounce of effort. This recipe requires less salt in the pasta cooking water than you'd normally add at the pre-salting stage. Ensure that you indent the gnocchi with a fork before cooking to encourage the sauce to really coat the pasta as you finish the dish off.

Serves 4

400g/14oz Salt-baked Squash
   flesh (de-seeded and skinned weight)
   (see page 173)
200g/7oz '00' flour, plus extra for
   rolling and shaping
1 egg, beaten
1 roasted red pepper
   (home-roasted or from a jar),
   de-seeded and roughly chopped
Handful of curly kale, roughly chopped
1 tbsp pine nuts
1 tbsp red pepper pesto
Glug of olive oil
Sea salt and cracked black pepper
Grated Parmesan cheese, to serve

Slice the cooled salt-baked squash in half, remove the seeds and skin, weigh out the quantity of flesh needed, then purée in a food processor with the flour and egg for 1–2 minutes. The mixture should form a fairly wet dough. It is generally moister than potato gnocchi, so don't be alarmed – if in doubt, add a little more flour until it is workable.

Tip out and knead the dough on a floured surface for a couple of minutes, then wrap and leave to chill in the fridge for 1 hour.

On a lightly floured surface, roll out the dough into roughly 3cm/1¼in diameter lengths and then slice across each to make bite-sized portions. Press a floured fork into each piece of gnocchi to indent – this allows the sauce to coat the gnocchi better when you fry them later.

Cook all of the squash gnocchi in a large saucepan of lightly salted boiling water for 2–3 minutes (or cook in batches if using a smaller pan) until they float to the surface.

Meanwhile, in a sauté pan, cook off the roasted pepper, kale, pine nuts and pesto with a glug of olive oil over a medium heat for a couple of minutes or so. Lift the cooked gnocchi across into the sauté pan with a slotted spoon and cook for a further 3–4 minutes until the gnocchi is golden and starting to crisp at the edges.

Serve with plenty of grated Parmesan and cracked black pepper.

Salt-baked Celeriac

In appearance, celeriac is straight out of a sci-fi film with gnarled alien skin and soil-crammed crevices and craters which shape the surface of this strange-looking vegetable. I want to shine a light on the enigma around salt baking a celeriac and explain why it is such an effective recipe to enhance its core root flavour.

Even as an experienced chef, I don't relish the simple task of peeling a celeriac, and then there's the challenge of knowing how to cook it to avoid discolouring the creamy flesh as it oxidises easily. Deftly achieving the correct balance of salt to amplify the nutty flavour without masking its delicate bittersweet profile is also a tough skill to master. But when you bake a whole celeriac for long enough in a salt crust, the skin slides off with a rub of your thumb. It becomes a joy to peel, revealing a wonderful soft, juicy flesh. The woody notes sweeten to cedar and the salt softens bitterness in a mirage. This is an iconic piece of salt craft to explore.

Serves 4

6 egg whites

315g/11oz Anglesey sea salt

100g/3½oz plain flour

1 tbsp grated (peeled) fresh
  horseradish root

1 medium celeriac, about 750g/1lb 10oz

Preheat the oven to 180°C fan/400°F/gas mark 6.

Make the salt crust. Whisk the egg whites into stiff peaks in a bowl, then fold in the salt, flour, 5 tablespoons of water and the horseradish.

Spoon a dollop of the salt crust mixture onto a roasting tray, then gently place the whole celeriac on top. Cover the celeriac with the remaining salt crust mixture using a spatula, ensuring there are no holes or gaps.

Bake in the oven for 4 hours until the celeriac inside is butter-soft (use a skewer to check) and the crust is rock hard and granary brown in colour.

Break open the salt crust and peel the celeriac. At this point, you can serve it simply sliced, or cut into chunks and sautéed in some brown butter with ground white pepper, or blitz the salt-baked celeriac with some sautéed shallots, veg stock and blue cheese to make a creamy soup.

Celeriac Scotch Eggs

The ultimate picnic food with a twist. This recipe is nutty, sweet, creamy and full of a mineral-salty warmth that positions it firmly in the family recipe archive under 'comfort food'. I'd happily eat one of these for breakfast, lunch or dinner in a restaurant or on a park bench.

Makes 4

280g/10oz peeled Salt-baked Celeriac
  (see page 177)
Handful of curly kale, blanched and
  finely chopped
1 tsp Dijon mustard
1 tsp chopped sage
1–3 tbsp plain flour, plus extra
  for dusting
2 eggs, beaten
1 leek, finely sliced
1 shallot, finely sliced
1 large king oyster mushroom, grated
40g/1½oz salted butter
4 large, rich-yolk eggs
100g/3½oz panko breadcrumbs
Sea salt and cracked black pepper
Vegetable oil, for deep-frying

Grate the peeled celeriac flesh and mix in a bowl with the blanched kale, mustard, sage, 1 tablespoon of the flour and a quarter of the two beaten eggs. Set aside.

Sauté the leek, shallot and mushroom with the butter in a frying pan over a medium heat for about 4–5 minutes until softened, then season with a little salt and some pepper. Combine the sautéed veg in the bowl with the celeriac mix, then blitz half of this mixture in a food processor. By hand, stir the blitzed mixture into the remaining celeriac mix in the bowl for extra texture, and season to taste. It shouldn't need much more salt.

Test the mix is firm enough to hold together in your hand without falling apart and add a little more flour and beaten egg, if required. Set aside.

Next, boil the whole eggs for 4 minutes (I like a runny yolk, but cook them for longer if you prefer hard-boiled eggs to wrap around), then cool under cold running water. When they are cool enough to handle, peel the eggs and then coat each one with a quarter of the celeriac mix and form into a ball. Next, dust the balls gently in flour, coat in some of the remaining beaten egg, then roll the coated eggs in breadcrumbs to coat. Repeat this coating process a second time if you want a deeper breadcrumb coating. Place on a plate and leave to rest in the fridge for 30–40 minutes.

Pour enough vegetable oil into a large, deep, heavy-based saucepan so it comes about a third of the way up the sides of the pan (or use a deep-fat fryer) and heat over a medium heat until it reaches 180°C/350°F (or until a small piece of bread dropped in browns within 30 seconds – you want it to quickly turn golden brown and bubble rather than absorb too much oil). Deep-fry the celeriac Scotch eggs, a couple at a time, for 3–4 minutes, turning every 30 seconds until the coating is crispy and golden. Using a slotted spoon, transfer the Scotch eggs to some kitchen paper to absorb the excess oil. Bring the oil back up to temperature and deep-fry the remaining two Scotch eggs in the same way. Serve warm or cold. These are delicious on their own or served simply with a raw celeriac remoulade or some ale chutney.

If serving cold, these Scotch eggs will keep in an airtight container in the fridge for up to 7 days.

Salt-baked Spring Onions

When I first read about the adventures of zero-waste chef Douglas McMaster baking carrots in compost, my initial response was he'd fermented into a full hipster-fashion victim. But having now tried my own version with salt, I understand that the point was about building confidence in the kitchen to experiment and re-write some of the classical rules we've inherited.

This recipe could be adapted to use waste coffee granules for salt-baked sweet potatoes, salt and used teabags for trout, or scraps of citrus rind and chilli seeds with salt to bake king prawns. I found my compost hummus gave off a sweet aroma and obvious earthy quality. This tickled me because, as an author, I'm guilty of over-using the word *earthy* when describing the taste of food, and for the first time in this dish the term took on a real meaning.

This serving suggestion is in part inspired by the Catalonian tradition of cooking calçots packed together over a fire and serving them with a Romesco sauce. I've taken the liberty of using a smoked salt for extra umami seasoning at the end and, instead of blending the almonds and peppers into a sauce, plating them up simply roasted and drizzled with a nutty extra virgin olive oil. The spring onions could be replaced with calçots or baby leeks and finished over the grill, once they are soft and succulent from the salty compost bake.

Serves 2

For the spring onions
250g/9oz homemade compost
    or peat-free compost from a
    garden centre
5 egg whites
250g/9oz *sel gris* or fine sea salt flakes
    for a delicate flavour
12 spring onions, both ends trimmed

To serve and garnish
Roasted red peppers (home-roasted
    or from a jar), de-seeded and sliced
Smoked almonds
Smoked salt
Extra virgin olive oil
Edible flowers (optional)

Preheat the oven to 200°C fan/425°F/gas mark 7.

For the spring onions, spread the compost out in a roasting tray and bake for 10 minutes to sterilise it, then leave to cool. Use the same oven temperature for baking the spring onions and line a baking tray with baking parchment.

In a bowl, whisk the egg whites to stiff peaks. Add the compost and the salt and mix together, then place a spoonful of this mix onto the baking tray. Spread it out with a spatula (wide enough so the spring onions all fit on top in a single layer), then lay the spring onions gently on top. Don't trim off the outer layer of the spring onions at this point, as you'll want to peel it off after baking to remove any salt and compost.

Cover the onions with all the remaining salt/compost mixture, ensuring there are no gaps. Bake for 45 minutes so that the spring onions soften inside the steaming salt crust.

Remove from the oven and peel back the salt crust once it is cool enough to handle, then brush off any excess salt/compost mix from the onions. Peel off the outer layer of each spring onion, then serve the onions on a bed of roasted peppers and smoked almonds. Season to taste with smoked salt and then drizzle with extra virgin olive oil. Garnish with edible flowers, if you have some to hand. Best enjoyed eaten in the garden!

Chapter Fourteen
Flavoured Salts

I hope this chapter will inspire you to have a go at making your own flavoured salt today. Once you have created a small pot yourself, you'll never look back and I promise that this nugget of salt craft will take you to new and exciting places.

One day, I hope that I can collate every flavoured salt I've ever created and write a follow-up book that has an A–Z of flavoured salts and blends. My professional job for a few years has been to come up with innovative salt blends for restaurants and supermarkets and it's never become a chore. The versatility of salt is unreal and it can be used to rack up another flavour dimension with the addition of herbs, spices or other ingredients that provide more depth. Mixing a vanilla pod and some caster sugar with salt makes a radical blend that works just as well for scallops as it does for crème brûlée; beetroot juice simply mixed with salt crystals and then dried in the oven is mind-blowingly beautiful to look at and tastes earthy, metallic and sweet.

What herbs can you see right now? Do you have any to hand in the kitchen? I am sitting in my garden studio looking at a mixed bed of flowers with rosemary, fennel, rocket, rhubarb and spring onions all within picking distance. I could capture the intense summer flavour of all these in a salt.

Mix It Up

There are a few ways to make your own flavoured salts at home. For me, a rough ratio of about 20:1 for salt and chilli and very strong spices, and 10:1 for salt and herb or citrus blends. I suggest using fine sea salt flakes for making most flavoured salt blends. The smaller flakes disperse well with spices and herbs and provide a more even level of seasoning. There are no set rules though, so it really is up to your personal preference; the more flavours you add, the more they will directly impact the taste when seasoning the food that you are cooking.

(Left) Prawns cooked with paprika, white wine and saffron salt.
(Above) Vanilla salt

Remember these aren't spice blends, so the mix will taste too salty if you use it too heavily.

To make flavoured salts, dry-mix the flavour ingredients in a bowl with the salt for an even distribution. You can make a syrup or reduction by placing a liquid in a saucepan on a low simmer until it starts to thicken and turn sticky. When it reduces in volume to about one third of the original volume, take the intense liquid flavours and mix with the salt (but ensure that you don't over saturate the blend, or you will end up dissolving the salt). The downside of making wet salt mixes is, obviously, that they are more moist.

Additionally, I often use a food processor to blitz raw fruit, veg and herbs or other more unusual cooking ingredients with salt until I have a fine blend packed with flavour. If you have introduced moisture to a salt, it's important to dry the salt blend before storing in an airtight container. I use a dehydrator with baking sheets for a couple of hours or a very low oven at around 70°C fan/195°F/ gas oven very low. For best results, why not make flavoured salts as a fresh weekly kitchen task? This way, you can constantly mix it up with new ideas and unusual ingredients. Cooking should be enjoyable and a flavoured salt is a bit like getting a new toy – play with it and have fun.

(Above) Chilli salt is perfect for seasoning squash and roasting with some sage.

Citrusy Rosemary Salt

Rosemary leaves can be finely chopped and mixed with salt, grated lemon zest and cracked black pepper for a mature seasoning, which is capable of amping up a chicken roasting on the grill, flavouring a breadcrumb for monktail scampi or sprinkled over a mushroom pizza with some chilli oil.

Spicy Fennel Salt

Fennel tops can be combined with salt and sugar along with a few crushed dried juniper berries, black peppercorns and some coriander seeds for a soft cure on fillets of rainbow trout.

Peppery Rocket Salt

A huge handful of rocket leaves and their flowers can be blitzed with salt for a peppery-tasting, green-coloured salt to season focaccia or sprinkle over a venison carpaccio with blue cheese.

Intriguing Rhubarb Salt

Rhubarb, well, I love this idea, but I've never thought of it until now! Can we make a pink salt that's sweet, sour and sharp, all at the same time? The answer is a definite yes! Cook the rhubarb with a little root ginger, caster sugar, lemon juice and cider vinegar to make a pink syrup, then strain it and, once cool, stir with sea salt flakes. Try this blushing delight with grilled pork chops, grilled mackerel, tuna and avocado ceviche, or to rim a whiskey and rhubarb sour cocktail.

Smoky Spring Onion Salt

Finally, spring onions – these would work using the Charcoal Salt (black leek ash) recipe on page 190. Char the spring onions on a bed of hot coals to form an allium-flavoured charcoal. Once cooked and fully burnt, the blackened onions can be dried and blitzed. Use this charcoal salt to season a Romesco sauce with a burnt allium flavour, or sprinkle on a Caprese salad.

My point is you can use just about anything to make a flavoured salt.

Food Waste

Salts are an awesome preservative, so if you are trying to reduce your food waste at home, think about making flavoured salts for your larder and spice cupboard. Literally anything can be saved from going in the bin and turned into a flavoured salt. The obvious ones include used coffee grinds which can be combined with some paprika, smoked chilli and barbecue spices; the dregs of a bottle of wine transformed into wine salt; leftover herbs that are past looking their best; or scraps of roasted root vegetables like beetroot or carrot that will make pop-art coloured salt. You can even dehydrate excess kimchi or kraut and grind into a seasoned powder to finish a dish with an umami whack of lactic-sour tanginess.

Seasonality

The seasons provide me with inspiration for salts all the time. Foraged ingredients offer a revolving carousel of colours and wild outdoor aromas. Give elderflower, wild garlic, gorse, pine or seaweed a try. Seasonal vegetables shine when matched with flavoured salts that emphasise their qualities, for example, sage salt with squash or lemon salt on asparagus.

Storage

All salt stores best in an airtight container or a sterilised glass jar, including flavoured salts, but they also need to be kept in the dark and, if you want to keep them for more than 2 months, make sure the additional ingredients are dried. I often use flavoured salts a full year later that have retained much of their flavour and visual appeal, but there's nothing quite like a freshly made flavoured salt for taste impact.

(Left) I couldn't resist trying rhubarb salt in the end... used here to cure some wild salmon and cooked with rock samphire and grilled asparagus.
(Right top) Gorse salt
(Right middle) Wild garlic salt
(Right bottom) Lots of lemon zest, cracked black pepper, chives and a pinch of ground turmeric – ridiculously tasty salt blend to use with chicken or roasted new potatoes.

Charcoal Salt (Black Leek Ash)

This is the most rock 'n' roll flavoured salt you can make. It tastes dark and mysterious and can be used to add drama to the simplest of dishes. Leek ash provides an allium pungency that breaks through the charcoal blanket and complements the bright briny notes from the salt. It is one of my favourite salts for its sheer simplicity and contrasts so effectively with the pearl white flakes.

Makes about 250g/9oz

2 leeks, left whole and untrimmed
(or you can bypass the charcoal-
making stage and sacrifice the leek
flavour by using 2 tbsp deactivated
charcoal powder)
225g/8oz sea salt flakes

Place the leeks over hot embers or cook them dirty (directly on the charcoal). Cook for at least 25–30 minutes, gently turning occasionally, until they are blackened all over.

Allow the leeks to cool before peeling off the outer burnt layer of leek ash from each leek. You can then return the leeks to char more layers or eat these softened internal parts with some butter and parsley.

Place these outer layers into a pestle and mortar or food processor with 1 tablespoon of the sea salt and grind into a fine powder.

Combine the leek ash charcoal (or charcoal powder) with the remaining sea salt flakes to form a black, volcanic-grey salt blend. Store in an airtight container in a cool, dark place for up to 12 months.

Serve with roasted beetroot, grilled vegetable kebabs or corn on the cob or with a cooked loin of venison and girolles.

(Right) Charcoal salt sprinkled on summer courgette bruschetta with basil and cherry tomatoes.

Black Garlic Salt

This salt tastes more Roman than Julius Caesar. I remember my first Caprese salad on an Italian beach in Anzio when on holiday and this is my version of it. Wake up your taste buds and give this flavoured salt a go.

Makes about 150g/5½oz

6 black garlic cloves
140g/5oz sea salt (I use *sel gris* –
    see Salt Choice below)

Make the salt by blitzing the black garlic cloves and salt in a food processor using the pulse button until fully incorporated.

Spread out and dry the black garlic salt on a baking sheet in a dehydrator for a few hours or on a lined baking tray in a preheated low oven at 100°C fan/250°F/gas mark ½ for 30 minutes–1 hour.

Cool, then store in an airtight container in a cool, dark place for up to 12 months.

Serve with cooked venison or duck, roasted beetroot or heritage tomatoes (see recipe on page 194).

Salt Choice:
Sel gris

I decided to use a crunchy *sel gris* for this recipe as I wanted the salt to pop with texture and provide bite on top of the tomatoes and buttery soft cheese (see recipe on page 194). If a salt combination has ever felt operatic, then this is the one. The result of the black garlic puréed into the salt crystals is an earthen terracotta, tinged with burnt umber, but the notes are transcendental, like grey morning light bouncing off sun-bleached walls and mosaic tiles.

Tomato and Garlic Salad

There is something special about seeing an array of ripe roasted tomatoes scattered with pungent black salt. It screams loudly of continental flavour and has a rustic drama that reverberates like hearing an ancient tale of good and evil.

This salad is everything I love about seasonal food. Long summer evenings spent with friends and family – serving it is like lighting a flaming torch and holding it aloft to announce an umami seasoned feast. Best enjoyed with a chunk of bread and a glass of good red wine.

Serves 4

For the tomatoes
Selection of mixed large heritage
   tomatoes and cherry vine tomatoes,
   approx. 1kg/2lb 4oz total weight
1 tbsp extra virgin olive oil, plus extra
   for drizzling
½ tsp Black Garlic Salt (see page 193)
½ tsp cracked black pepper
8–12 basil leaves
1 bulb roasted garlic, separated into
   cloves with papery skins left on
1 tbsp capers in brine or vinegar,
   drained

To serve
1 burrata or mozzarella ball, drained
   and torn into pieces
Basil leaves
1 tbsp balsamic glaze
Small pinch of Black Garlic Salt
   (see page 193)
Focaccia or toasted ciabatta

Preheat the oven to 200°C fan/425°F/gas mark 7.

Slice the larger tomatoes in half and then arrange all of the tomatoes on a baking tray. Drizzle with the measured olive oil and season with the black garlic salt and black pepper. Tear the fresh basil leaves over the tomatoes and squeeze the roasted garlic cloves into the gaps. Add the capers, then roast for 15–20 minutes until the tomatoes have softened and are starting to char in places.

Serve warm with the burrata or mozzarella pieces and basil leaves. Drizzle with a little more olive oil, the balsamic glaze and a small pinch of black garlic salt. Serve with focaccia or toasted ciabatta.

Chicken Salt

A pinch of chicken salt transforms a piece of cod (see recipe on page 198) and it's delicious on sliced avocado with lemon juice, on chicken kebabs to pop on the barbie, or for a chicken butter.

This salt is also a great zero-waste way to use chicken skin from a roast, although in my house, there's hardly ever any leftover skin, so this recipe needs huge self-restraint when carving the bird and returning the skin to the oven to crisp up instead of eating it.

You can make 100 per cent chicken skin salt and I often do, but I like the Aussie-style chicken salt, too, which is often vegetarian and made from spices and seasoning.

This mixture of some more commercial flavours combined with carefully roasted chicken skin is my idea of guilty-pleasure heaven.

Makes about 200g/7oz

2 chicken breast skins
6 tbsp Himalayan fine salt
2 tbsp chicken stock powder
2 tbsp garlic powder
1 tbsp sweet paprika
1 tsp onion powder
½ tsp ground white pepper

Preheat the oven to 200°C fan/425°F/gas mark 7.

Place the chicken skins on a baking tray between two sheets of baking parchment and sandwich with another baking tray on top to keep it weighted down. Roast for 20–22 minutes until golden and crispy.

Allow to cool on a wire rack. Once cool, blitz with the Himalayan salt and all the remaining ingredients in a food processor into a fine blend. Store in an airtight container in the fridge for up to 2–3 weeks.

Serve with chips, roast chicken, mac 'n' cheese or salt and pepper chicken wings.

Cod with Chicken Butter Sauce, Braised Cabbage and Asparagus

This is my most subtle surf 'n' turf recipe, but like the sea, hidden beneath the serene appearance are lashings of powerful umami seasoning. The elegant combination of chicken salt, butter and cod is a form of quiet magic for the tongue, paired with fruity braised cabbage and tender asparagus spears. Try this combination and you will forever yearn for chicken salt with your cod. It's a match that conjures up memories of peaceful walks along the seashore.

Serves 2

For the braised cabbage and steamed asparagus

55g/2oz salted butter

1 Chinese cabbage, sliced lengthways
    into segments

125ml/4fl oz dry cider

Pinch of Chicken Salt (see page 197)

6 asparagus spears, trimmed

For the cod

1 tbsp olive oil

2 cod fillets, skin removed

25g/1oz unsalted butter, diced

1 tbsp chopped dill

Pinch of Chicken Salt (see page 197)

For the braised cabbage, melt the butter in a non-stick frying pan and sear the cabbage over a high heat for 2–3 minutes. Add the cider, cover with a lid and leave to braise over a low heat for 15 minutes. Season with the chicken salt just before serving. Meanwhile, steam the asparagus for 3–4 minutes.

When the cabbage is nearly ready, cook the cod. Heat the olive oil in another non-stick frying pan and place the cod fillets into the pan. Cook over a medium-high heat for 3 minutes on each side and add the butter, dill and chicken salt when you turn the fish. The cod should become opaque, flaky, moist and well seasoned with the chicken salt while cooking in the butter.

Serve the cod with the cabbage and asparagus and a cold crisp glass of cider or light hoppy IPA with citrus notes.

Truffle Salt

When cooked with love, a mushroom risotto is always delicious and creamy. But when you add a pinch of truffle salt, the dish builds tree houses in the soul. A small amount of truffle goes a long way and preserves the flavour for the seasons ahead.

Makes about 250g/9oz

½ fresh black truffle, finely chopped

250g/9oz sea salt flakes
  (I use *fleur de sel*)

½ tsp porcini powder

Using a dehydrator, dehydrate the truffle pieces at 50–60°C/122–140°F for about 8 hours.

Leave to cool, then combine with the sea salt flakes and porcini powder. Blitz in a small food processor to break up the truffle and disperse it into the salt fully.

Keep in an airtight container in a cool, dark place for up to 12 months to retain the gorgeous smell. Serve with mushrooms on toast, cooked eggs, risotto (see recipe below), fungi pizza or fresh figs.

A Truffle-y Mushroom Risotto

These rustic flavours taste of home comfort. The simple addition of truffle salt to season this recipe takes it from a hearty meal in a woodland cabin to the top table at a palace feast.

Serves 2

4 tbsp grated Parmesan cheese

1 tbsp truffle oil, plus an extra drizzle

175g/6oz wild mushrooms, diced

1 shallot, finely diced

1 garlic clove, diced

1 tbsp dried porcini, diced

115g/4oz Arborio rice

50ml/2fl oz masala wine

1 litre/1¾ pints hot chicken stock

1 tbsp finely chopped chives

3–4 pinches of Truffle Salt
  (see above)

2 pinches of cracked black pepper

1 king oyster mushroom, sliced and
  lightly scored with a cross-hatch cut

Preheat the oven to 200°C fan/425°F/gas mark 7 and line a baking tray with baking parchment.

To make the Parmesan crisps, make two heaped circles of the grated cheese (each about 10cm/4in in diameter) on the lined baking tray and bake for 12 minutes until they have spread out and turned golden brown. Allow to cool on the baking tray until solid, then carefully peel each one off the paper. Set aside.

Meanwhile, make a classic mushroom risotto but start by using the truffle oil for the wild mushrooms, shallot and garlic. Sauté in a saucepan over a medium heat for 5–10 minutes until softened, then add in the dried porcini and rice followed by the wine.

Deglaze the risotto pan, then add in a ladleful of hot stock at a time, allowing the rice to soak it up before adding the next one. Continue gradually adding the stock in this way and cooking for about 20 minutes until the rice softens but retains a little nutty bite. Toss with the chives and season with a pinch each of truffle salt and black pepper.

Meanwhile, sear the sliced oyster mushroom in a non-stick frying pan with a drizzle of truffle oil and another pinch each of truffle salt and black pepper. Cook over a high heat until golden, about 8 minutes.

Plate up the risotto on the pan-fried mushroom slices and garnish each portion with a Parmesan crisp. Finish with a final pinch of truffle salt.

Roast Salt

Taking on the Great British Roast was a challenge I invented for myself a few years back when I was creating seasoning blends for a job. I tried to represent an occasion with a seasoning – this is no inconsiderable feat to attempt and there were a couple of versions before this one. But now I know that this salt really works because, like taking coals to Manchester or selling pasties to Cornishmen, I took my recipe up North and made a roast with a renowned maker of Yorkshire puddings. It got their seal of approval.

The seasoning really works on roast chicken, all sorts of potatoes, as well as root vegetables and delivers a nostalgic sprinkle to gatherings at a long table. Try it in my delicious Yorkshire Puddings, too (see page 205).

Makes about 100g/3½oz

70g/2½oz sea salt flakes
(I use *fleur de sel de Île de Ré* –
see Salt Choice on page 205)
1 tsp grated (peeled) fresh
horseradish root
1 tsp cracked black pepper
½ tsp garlic powder
½ tsp onion powder
½ tsp dried rosemary
½ tsp ground bay
½ tsp dried sage

Combine all the ingredients in a bowl. Blitz this blend well in a food processor, then store in an airtight container in a cool, dark place for up to 12 months.

Yorkshire Puddings

Elevating a Yorkshire Pudding batter is a challenge, but I honestly believe that this recipe helps take a much-loved family favourite to the next level. The salt and roast dinner-inspired herbs and spices work well at building a steady background noise to the Yorkshire's flavour profile – like a low-level chatter, bubbling away at the dinner table when families gather around to share stories. It's hard to pin down when you are in the moment, but it's greatly missed when it's not there.

Serves 6 (makes 12 individual puddings)

4 eggs

200ml/7fl oz whole milk

140g/5oz plain flour

1 tsp Roast Salt (see page 202)

Beef dripping or vegetable oil, for cooking

Preheat the oven to 200°C fan/425°F/gas mark 7.

Whisk the eggs in a bowl until fluffy, then slowly pour in the milk. Beat until smooth, then gradually add a spoonful of flour at a time, whisking until you have a smooth batter. Stir in the roast salt seasoning and transfer to a jug.

Place ½ teaspoon of dripping or oil into each of the holes of two 6-cup muffin trays (or use one 12-cup muffin tray) and heat in the oven for 3 minutes.

Once the fat is smoking hot, remove from the oven and pour the Yorkshire batter evenly into the trays.

Return the trays to the oven and cook for 25 minutes until risen and golden. Do not open the oven while cooking, as this will collapse the Yorkshires. Serve warm for an ultimate roast dinner.

Salt Choice:

Fleur de sel

I use a *fleur de sel de Île de Ré* for my roast salt, as I like the way it has a fine crystal grain but is still packed with mineral flavour and a brave bitterness that stands up to peppery heat. You could also try a version of this recipe using a smoked salt and make a heavier barbecue roasting salt with a pinch of light soft brown sugar added in. Alternatively, try lightening the roast salt with dried tarragon instead of sage, adding a little grated lemon zest, or adding more garlic powder and a pinch of ground mace for a roasting salt that's perfect for chicken and fish.

Mint Salt

This verdant minted salt seasons food with a sun-kissed wave of grassy flavour. I used to make a version that combined mint, fennel seeds and lemon zest in the blend, but I think that this stripped-back blend is an improvement for its sheer simplicity and versatility. Minted salt is a larder staple to keep on making from fresh garden mint all season long.

Use it with diced cantaloupe melon and blue cheese in a salad, sprinkled over grilled scallops with pea purée, or to season pan-fried lamb chops (see recipe opposite) or roasted vegetables and baked feta.

Makes about 150g/5½oz

8 sprigs mint, leaves picked

140g/5oz sea salt crystals

Blitz the mint and salt in a food processor until you have a smooth green colour. You can dry the salt in a dehydrator or on a baking tray in a low oven at 70°C fan/195°F/gas oven very low to increase the shelf life, but it sacrifices some of the brightness. I tend to store it fresh in an airtight container in a cool, dry place and use within 2 weeks.

Mustard-glazed Lamb Chops

Herby goodness – oh me, oh my, how spring lamb loves mint. This superfly flavoured salt is a sure-fire way to bring some joy to a simple chop.

Serves 4

8 small lamb cutlets, about
   650g/1lb 7oz in total

1 tsp Mint Salt (see opposite),
   plus an extra pinch

½ tsp cracked black pepper

125ml/4fl oz dry cider

1 tbsp wholegrain mustard

2 tbsp runny honey

55g/2oz unsalted butter

4 garlic cloves, bashed in their skins

To serve

Boiled potatoes with fresh mint

Roasted tomatoes

Chargrilled baby leeks

Season the lamb chops on both sides with the mint salt and black pepper. Cook the lamb in a large, non-stick pan over a medium-high heat and render the fat down for 4–5 minutes until golden. Turn the chops on their side and cook for 2 more minutes.

Meanwhile, in a small saucepan, reduce the cider, mustard and honey over a high heat for 5 minutes until sticky. Set aside.

Add the butter and garlic to the lamb pan and cook until golden and bubbly, at the same time searing the chops for a further 1–2 minutes on each side.

Brush the chops with a glaze of the reduced cider, mustard and honey mixture. Remove from the heat, cover with foil and allow to rest for 5–10 minutes.

Season the lamb with one final pinch of mint salt before serving with the selection of vegetables.

Red Wine Salt

Every wine salt will taste slightly different depending on what wine and which salt you use for your recipe. The basic method can be applied with any drink, and once you've tried this recipe, give coffee salt or elderflower cordial salt a try. The key is to mix the salt with enough wine to coat it evenly and create a wet sand consistency that's moist to touch but not so much that it dissolves the salt. Choosing salt crystals rather than flakes also helps.

I make this flavoured salt completely by eye and feel. Don't be afraid to have a go – you will be amazed at the results and you'll never waste the dregs of the wine bottle again. A clever way to improve the intensity of flavour is to reduce the wine first in a pan over a medium-low heat for 20–30 minutes to make a syrup, then leave to cool slightly before combining it with salt.

After you have made your wine salt, I recommend taking time to dry it properly before using and storing in an airtight container. It goes without saying that you probably need to make both a red and white wine salt for your larder – for the sake of science, of course.... When choosing wines, try bold, full-bodied bottles and robust fruity flavours. From personal experience, a Rioja, Chianti or Merlot works well for red wine salt, and you can't go wrong with an oak-aged Chardonnay for white wine salt.

Makes about 150g/5½oz

150ml/¼ pint Merlot
115g/4oz sea salt crystals

Reduce the wine in a saucepan over a high heat for 10–15 minutes until it forms a slightly thicker syrup. Allow to cool slightly, then gently stir the salt crystals into the wine syrup to coat evenly.

Transfer to a baking tray and dry in a preheated oven at 150°C fan/ 340°F/gas mark 3½ for 25–30 minutes, or dry overnight in a dehydrator at 50°C/122°F.

Cool, then store in an airtight container in a cool, dark place for up to 12 months.

Serve with sliced bresaola, cooked beef short rib, chorizo or lamb chops, dirty onions (see recipe on page 211) or rosemary-roasted potatoes.

Dirty Onions with Red Wine Salt

I think that dirty onions with red wine salt mingling at a party could become
a thing. It's a dish that's easy to cook, delightful to look at and a pleasure
to eat. The red wine salt adds a tannic, fruit-laden seasoning to the smoky,
sweet onions, and unsalted butter and parsley introduce the two parts with a
polite ease.

Serves 4

8 red onions in their skins

85g/3oz unsalted butter

4 tbsp finely sliced parsley

Large pinch of Red Wine Salt
(see page 208)

Edible flowers, such as French
marigolds or calendula (optional)

Roast the onions in their skins over a wood fire or on a bed of hot
charcoal – you can cook these dirty straight on the coals or on an open
grill. Cook for 25–30 minutes, occasionally turning them carefully, until
completely blackened all over.

Inside, the onions will be soft and succulent. Slice each one in half and
pull the cooked onion out of the charred outer layer. Put the cooked
onions in a serving dish and discard the charred outer layers.

Gently melt the butter and parsley together in a pan and then pour
over the onions. Season generously with the red wine salt, then serve
with some edible flowers, if you have them.

Red Salt

Bring some fire to your seasoning. I think that sometimes it is important to cater to a fiery palate. Make sure that the red salt is spicy enough so that your guests don't have to add too much salt in search of delivering that addictive Scoville heat. There's nothing worse than a mild chilli salt that then risks over-seasoning a recipe as you try to tease out the warmth. It's far safer to have an extremely spicy red salt and to use less of it. This is pretty grown-up, so keep it out of reach of children.

Makes about 45g/1½oz

2 tbsp red Alaea salt
  (see Salt Choice below)
1 tsp dried chilli flakes
1 tsp dried smoked chilli flakes
1 tsp Cajun spice blend
½ tsp dried red pepper flakes

Mix the red Alaea salt with the combination of chilli flakes, the Cajun spice blend and red pepper flakes. You can tailor this blend to suit what chilli you have available, but remember that it really can afford to be punchy and on the spicy side. Store in an airtight container in a cool, dry place for up to 12 months.

Serve with gumbo (see recipe opposite), cooked king prawns, carnitas or chilli con carne.

Salt Choice:

Alaea

I love the deep pepper-red hue and earthy flavour of red Alaea salt and it provides a fantastic colour to this flavoured blend. The reddish colour results from iron oxide found naturally in the Hawaiian clay (renowned for its health benefits) which is then mixed with unrefined sea salt.

Jimmy's Jumbo Gumbo

This recipe came straight off a menu at a BBQ Smokehouse pop-up restaurant that I ran for a couple of years at festivals. I only have one friend who calls me Jimmy, but this seems to be an appropriate name for the dish. Be generous, invite friends, have fun and make your red salt naughty.

Serves 4

For the gumbo

3 celery sticks, diced

1 red pepper, de-seeded and sliced

2 shallots, diced

1 tbsp Cajun spice blend

1 tsp fennel seeds

2 tbsp olive oil

4 fresh chorizo sausages
   (about 400g/14oz in total)

55g/2oz cured chorizo, diced

2 skinless, boneless chicken
   breasts, diced

1 tbsp plain flour

1 bulb roasted garlic, separated
   into cloves and flesh squeezed out

850ml/1½ pints chicken stock

2 tbsp hot pepper sauce

175g/6oz raw peeled king prawns

1 tsp Red Salt (see page 212), plus
   extra to serve

For the dirty rice

280g/10oz basmati rice

225g/8oz (drained weight) tinned
   black beans, drained and rinsed

2 tbsp chopped coriander

2 tbsp crispy onions

Pinch of Red Salt (see page 212),
   or to taste

Start by cooking the gumbo trio of celery, red pepper and shallots in the Cajun spice blend and fennel seeds with the oil and both the chorizos in a saucepan. Sauté over a medium-high heat for 5–10 minutes until browned, then add the chicken, flour and roast garlic flesh. Cook out the flour to darken into a sticky brown roux base and then stir in the chicken stock and hot pepper sauce.

Bring the gumbo back to a simmer and then reduce the heat. Cook, uncovered, for 15–20 minutes until thick and bubbling away nicely, then add the prawns. Cook for a further 5–6 minutes until the prawns are cooked through. Season with the red salt and serve with extra at the table. You will only be seasoning the gumbo a little because the cured chorizo and sausages in the dish itself will taste fairly salty.

Meanwhile, for the dirty rice, cook the rice in a separate pan of boiling water for 12–15 minutes until fluffy and tender, then drain and return to the pan. Mix in the black beans, coriander and crispy onions and warm through over a medium heat for 2–3 minutes. Season with red salt to taste and serve the rice with a ladleful of gumbo for each portion.

Chapter Fifteen
Smoked Salt

Smoked salt is my cooking sweetheart, my seasoning darling. I've loved smoked food since the age of ten years old when I built my first smoker with my dad. We used to cold smoke cheese and hard-boiled eggs over oak shavings in the back garden using a rusty, burnt-out oil drum.

For me, there's a primal pull that gathers friends close to the heart of a campfire in the dark, drawing a tight crowd to the grill at a family barbecue, vying for position with tongs and beer in hand. Smoked food tastes elemental, dark, woody and intense. I would go so far as to say smoked salt is a completely different branch of seasoning.

How Smoke Works

If you want to smoke salt and incorporate it into your food, you will need both patience and a smoker. Cold smoking works best between 15–30°C/59–86°F – this temperature range matters less with salts compared to smoked food, but I find it's still the best flavour region for smoke compounds. Immense flavour is imparted when cold smoking that further dries the salt and removes moisture before storing. Always smoke salt for long periods of time – you will get best results smoking salt for between 24–48 hours.

I recommend smoking salt with oak, apple, mesquite or cherry wood for fruity notes that work well with a bright-tasting salt. You could also use maple, beech, hickory or olive or even try something more unusual and smoke with herbs. The flavours change from wood to wood. The three main compounds in wood are cellulose, hemicellulose and lignin, and the balance of these will differ from wood to wood, hence the subtle differences in flavour. As they combust, they release sweet, caramel-like flavour molecules. You get particularly spicy notes from the lignin, as it breaks down into phenolics which are volatile flavour compounds providing the smoky notes. Oak and hickory have particularly high levels of lignin and, therefore, add more flavour and smokier tones to salt as a result.

These aromatic compounds will adhere to the surface of the salt. To replace the pellicle, which is the tacky texture on cured meats and fish that helps the smoke stick, I recommend ever so slightly moistening the salt before putting it into the smoker. It will dry, but the moisture can help smoke bond to the surface of the flakes. Also make sure that you spread the salt out in a shallow layer and turn or stir it after the first day in the smoker.

Choosing a Cold Smoker

Cold smokers come in all shapes and sizes and there is a wide range available to buy. Alternatively, you can easily try making your own.

The key requirement for cold smoking is a cabinet where you can contain the smoke but allow some airflow for the wood shavings, sawdust or wood chips to burn and for smoke to circulate (I tend to use fine wood shavings or sawdust for cold smoking as they have a larger surface area and stay lit for longer, and I use larger wood shavings, wood chips or wooden blocks for hot smoking). You could use an old whiskey barrel with some racks in the middle, a door at the bottom and some holes drilled in the top. I've seen cold smokers made with an old fridge and a large wooden shed – the possibilities are endless.

Removable racks are important for easy cleaning. Ice trays in the lower layers keep the smoker cold, but this tends to be more important for smoking dairy and fish. The smoke can be generated directly beneath the salt and diffused with a simple baffle of some sort, so that it spreads out as it rises, or you can have a separate fire chamber connected by a flue for the cold smoke to then rise into the smoking chamber. A cold-smoke generator is a fantastic gadget – it allows the wood shavings or sawdust to burn in a slow coil over 10–12 hours or longer (refilling it if necessary to keep a steady smoke). If you don't have one of these, then arrange the wood shavings/sawdust in a large spiral and light one end for them to smoke for a longer period.

How to Smoke Salt

Smoked salt is almost its own genre of seasoning. The smoky aroma and lightly stained flakes are superb for adding depth of flavour and an authentic smoked taste to all sorts of foods from eggs to butter. I reach for my smoked salt almost daily when cooking. It's the easiest salt hack to master and to give your cooking variety and punch. To me, it's like building a bassline of flavour into recipes that provides a driving rhythm across a plate of food like a metronome ticking between sweet, spicy and smoked to play together with a country grace.

Makes about 200g/7oz

200g/7oz sea salt flakes
2–4 cups wood sawdust or fine
    wood shavings

Spread out the salt in a single layer on a sheet of foil on a small, shallow metal baking tray so it's in as thin a layer as possible (or you can use a fine-mesh stainless-steel sieve that fits inside the smoker).

Place the salt into the cold smoker and light the cold-smoke generator (if you don't have one, see page 215) filled with the sawdust/wood shavings. Smoke for 24–48 hours, stirring every few hours. You can cold smoke salt for up to 14 days for a really strong smoky aroma. Refill the cold-smoke generator every 12 hours or so for a slow steady smoke. How far you take your smoked salt is completely up to you. Try a long slow smoke with plenty of sawdust/wood shavings or a shorter smoking time for a lighter finish. Personally, I like smoking some salts with an intense, dark wood smoke using oak or hickory, but I also like having a light apple smoked salt available for seafood dishes and for serving with scrambled eggs. Try both and see what you prefer.

Leave the smoked salt to cool, then store in an airtight container in a cool, dark place for up to 12 months.

Try using smoked salt in barbecue seasoning rubs, to rim cocktails or as a finishing salt with an extra boost of umami.

Whiskey-smoked Barbecue Salt

This smoked salt captures my memory of all things warm and peaty and takes me back to when I stay with my Irish granny and am treated to a couple of fingers of whiskey in an Antrim-cut crystal glass with a drop of water, while watching *The Quiet Man*. The tangy smoked salt in this sea salt blend cuts through the sweet, woody flavours of the spices and is so cowboy it makes you feel as if John Wayne is right there in your kitchen shouting to you to 'get off your horse and drink your milk'. It's worth mixing this smoked salt with my barbecue spices to give you that authentic saloon twang, ragtime blues banging out from a bashed-up old piano in the corner. Release your inner Billy the Kid and have a go at smoking salt with whiskey barrel offcuts.

I use flakes for this smoked salt because they taste like bacon crumbs when you rub them onto steaks, but you could also try this technique with traditional salt crystals.

Makes about 200g/7oz smoked salt;
Makes about 125g/4½oz barbecue rub

For the whiskey-smoked sea salt

4–6 lumps of whiskey or bourbon
   barrel offcuts

200g/7oz sea salt flakes

For the barbecue rub

4 tbsp Whiskey-smoked Sea Salt
   (see above)

2 tbsp demerara sugar

2 tbsp smoked paprika

1 tbsp onion powder

1 tbsp garlic powder

1 tsp ground white pepper

1 tsp smoked chilli/chipotle powder

1 tsp coriander seeds, crushed
   or ground

1 tsp hot chilli powder

1 tsp dried red pepper flakes

1 tsp ground ginger

1 tsp dried thyme

Light the cold smoker with the barrel offcuts and allow the smoke to get established while you line a small, shallow metal baking tray with foil (or use a fine-mesh stainless-steel sieve that fits inside the smoker) and then sprinkle over the sea salt flakes in a thin layer.

Smoke the salt for 8–12 hours, stirring the salt every few hours so it all gets exposed to the smoke for an even finish. For this recipe, you could also hot smoke the salt with the wood offcuts for 1–2 hours in a vertical stack hot smoker or a kettle barbecue.

Once smoked, allow the salt to cool, then store in an airtight container in a cool, dark place for up to 12 months. Use it with mackerel fillets on the grill, sprinkled over scrambled eggs or for a chilli con carne. It's even delicious with guacamole or tomatoes on toast.

To make the barbecue rub, measure out the amount of whiskey-smoked salt required, then mix it with all the remaining ingredients in a small bowl for a fantastic, versatile barbecue rub. Store in an airtight container in a cool, dark place for up to 3 months. Use it with ribs, sweetcorn or chicken wings or lightly sprinkled onto steaks. This barbecue rub is also fantastic with sweet potato fries or ember-roasted hasselback squash.

Seaweed-smoked Salt

A few years ago, my mum and her husband Rob returned from an epic trip around the Outer Hebrides in their campervan with a very special bottle for my wife and I to enjoy. It was an artisan gin flavoured with seaweed – the bottle was a pale, oceanic blue with twisted waves of rippled glass and it tasted as good as it looked. It had never occurred to me before to use seaweed in something so distilled and clean. Since then, I've been hooked on seaweed-infused drinks. Recently, I even had a rum flavoured with smoked dulse that was fantastic, so I decided to start cold smoking seaweed to flavour my salt.

Keep some seaweed-smoked salt next to your barbecue and try it next time you are grilling some lobster or cooking salt lamb. The seaweed salt is brilliant with beef burgers for an umami seasoning.

Makes about 200g/7oz

4 large handfuls of freshly foraged
    seaweed (see method)
140g/5oz sea salt flakes
Few handfuls of apple wood shavings
    (optional)

Start by foraging for a few large handfuls of seaweed. Try to get a good mixture for the first blend. As you become more familiar with the varieties of seaweed, you could perfect a specific smoke with something like pepper dulse for a powerful truffle smoked flavour, or dulse to enhance the strong, fried bacon taste profile.

Cut the seaweed at low tide from the rocks rather than using any floating seaweed, which is dead and may not be healthy. All seaweed is edible, so you can safely gather from areas with clean seawater (see the 'Making Salt' section in chapter 1 on pages 22-3 for guidance).

Take the seaweed home and dry it in the sun for a couple of days or overnight in a dehydrator at 55°C/131°F or overnight in a low fan oven at 50°C fan/158°F/very low gas oven. You can also leave seaweed to dry on an air-drying hanger/airer in a well-ventilated, dry room at home. When it is dry, arrange it inside a cold smoker or a kettle barbecue where you would normally place the wood chips/shavings/sawdust and carefully light it with a blowtorch or natural firelighter to start smoking the salt. Once the seaweed is generating a good amount of smoke, after 5–10 minutes, add the salt to be smoked.

Make sure the salt is spread out in a thin layer over a small, shallow, foil-lined metal baking tray or in a fine-mesh stainless steel sieve and place it in the cold smoker or kettle barbecue. Cover the smoker/barbecue with a lid and leave to smoke for 4–8 hours (see next step). Check that the seaweed is still alight every hour or so – mine tends to need some attention at intervals, as Cornwall can be pretty damp, so it takes the seaweed here a long time to dry fully. If it goes out, then add a few handfuls of apple wood shavings to help keep it smoking nicely. Stir the layer of salt every couple of hours so all the flakes are exposed to the smoke for an even finish.

The longer you smoke the salt for, the more pronounced the smoked flavour, so it's completely up to you to say when enough is enough. I like a gentle level of seaweed smoke to use in my seafood cookery, so 4–5 hours smoking is often my preference. If you smoke for longer lengths of time, you can achieve an almost bacon, beef-jerky smoke level that is caramel-sweet and sticky. Try the salt every few hours and extend the smoking time depending on your personal taste. This type of cooking is refreshingly instinctive and allows you to create smoked salts that are tuned to your individual tastes.

When the salt is ready, allow it to cool, then store in an airtight container in a cool, dark place for up to 12 months.

Use with grilled cos lettuce, sea vegetables, monkfish tails or chicken wings or roasted John Dory. This recipe is almost so tasty that a part of me doesn't even want to share it with you! Enjoy!

Smoked Salted Butter

Buttery gold seems an appropriate description for this recipe. Smoked salt is special to me as I'm a massive fan of cooking and smoking over fire and, as a chef, I'm biased, but I believe butter makes all food taste better – it genuinely brings me joy to cook with freshly-churned butter. If you are also a fan of butter, then this recipe will only fuel your passion for the ingredient – making your own butter is remarkably straightforward.

Makes 1 pat of butter

For the smoked salt and garlic
115g/4oz sea salt flakes
2 garlic bulbs, left whole
4 tbsp wood shavings
   (I recommend either oak, apple
   or cherry), plus extra for longer
   smoking times

For the smoked salted butter
1 litre/1¾ pints double cream
1 tbsp smoked garlic purée
   (see above and method)
½ tsp Smoked Sea Salt (see page 216)

Cold smoke the salt and garlic for 24–48 hours using the wood shavings to generate a steady amount of smoke over the 1–2 days (replenishing with additional wood shavings periodically, if required). To do this, once the smoker is piping away, spread the salt in a thin layer over a small, shallow, foil-lined metal baking tray or, better still, spread it in a fine-mesh stainless-steel sieve, and place on a shelf in the smoker. Place the garlic bulbs on another shelf in the smoker. Stir the salt a few times during smoking to bring the buried flakes to the top and achieve an even smoke across the surface.

Once both the salt and garlic are smoked and have taken on bucket-loads of flavour, make the butter.

Remove the cream from the fridge an hour beforehand. Whip in a bowl with electric beaters until it reaches stiff peaks, then continue to beat further until the butter forms. It will start to appear yellow and, as part of the churning process, will change to the texture of scrambled eggs. At this point, the buttermilk will separate from the butter-fat solids. Drain the buttermilk away – it makes great pancakes or can be used to brine chicken wings (see recipe on page 108).

Rinse the solid butter under cold running water and then squeeze out any remaining buttermilk with butter pats or two spatulas. Use a piece of cheesecloth or muslin to dry off the butter.

Separate the smoked garlic bulbs into cloves and squeeze the flesh out of the papery skins. Blitz the smoked garlic flesh in a food processor or finely chop and then grind into a purée using a pestle and mortar. Measure out the tablespoon needed for this recipe and keep the rest in an airtight container or sterilised jar in the fridge covered with a little olive oil – it will keep in the fridge for up to 1 month.

Mix the measured garlic purée and the smoked salt with the freshly churned butter in a bowl. Form the butter into a pat or serve fresh.

The smoked butter will keep in an airtight container in the fridge for up to 14 days. It can also be rolled in baking parchment and stored in the freezer for up to 2 months. It can be used from frozen in recipes or defrosted to serve at the table with fresh bread.

Try this butter with grilled fish, on sourdough, added to scrambled eggs or in a mussel dish with pancetta, cider and thyme.

Smoked Seawater

Liquid seasoning in smoked water just makes sense to me. Smoke and salt, as you may have gathered from my love letters in this section, are special to me. What I love most about smoked seawater is that it is not singular. It can't be put in a little box and allocated one single application. In fact, the incredible part of it is no one has written the rules yet on how you should use it – you could add it to brines, cocktails, marinades, sauces or dressings.

This smoky seasoning is super versatile and fun to use. My top recommendations are to try adding some drops to a hot toddy, use it for wet curing short ribs ahead of slow roasting them with horseradish salt and a sticky beer barbecue glaze, or to dress heritage tomatoes with herb oil and roasted garlic.

Makes about 2 litres/3½ pints

2 litres/3½ pints clean seawater
(see the 'Making Salt' section in
chapter 1 on pages 22-3 for
guidance on collecting clean
seawater)
Oak wood sawdust or fine shavings

Filter the water by gently pouring it through a sieve lined with cheesecloth or muslin into a bowl. Allow to settle for 1–2 hours, then pour into a shallow roasting tray.

Light the cold smoker with a cold-smoke generator (if you don't have one, see page 215) filled with oak wood sawdust or fine shavings. Place the roasting tray into the smoker and cold smoke for 24–48 hours.

Cool the smoked water, then store in an airtight container or sterilised glass bottle in the fridge for up to 1 month.

Salt Geek

Instead of smoking the seawater yourself, you could also simply dissolve smoked sea salt into tap water at 2–3 per cent. This way you will get some very subtle smoked flavour but nowhere near as much as when smoking the water yourself.

Chapter Sixteen
Baking

Salt is a minor ingredient in bread, but it has a massive impact on its quality. The role salt plays in bread making is essential to the pace of fermentation and the development of structure (i.e. the way gluten proteins develop in dough) and it's pivotal to enhancing flavour and, ultimately, to baking a tasty bread.

Seasoning dough, like fermentation, is one of the few areas of cooking where complete precision can make a big difference to the end result. Exact measurements can be worth really paying attention to. Personally, I still prefer to bake primarily by eye. This is instinctive and takes practice to get a feel for a certain recipe, and I'll happily confess I've made a few mistakes over the years. The same goes for under-salting bread or over-seasoning dough. It's easily done but there is a considered, quietly spoken, sweet spot at between 1.8–2.2 per cent weight of salt to quantity of flour. Always aim for this percentage and you can't go far wrong.

I'm a self-confessed tactile baker, relying on experience and instinct rather than always following a recipe to the letter. Recipes are great guidelines, but remember that everyone has different ingredients: the sourdough starter may have a slightly different hydration and flours have their own character or at least they should do, especially heritage grains and wholewheat varieties, which can differ quite a lot depending on how finely they are milled and what water they can hold. All yeasts will respond differently from kitchen to kitchen due to warmth and hydration. Really tasty food requires your personal attention rather than a factory recipe card.

For baking at home, I add salt to bread with my eyes and fingers, rather than using scales. It should be a great testing ground for learning to season consistently and with confidence. The flour, yeast and water should remain the same while you use breads as a space to practise how to season with skill. Get yourself a set of micro-kitchen scales that can measure by the gram. Weigh out the salt once for a standard loaf recipe. Handle it, let it run through your fingers and then sprinkle into the flour before kneading with the yeasty water. The next time, forget the scales and trust yourself. That's how I love to season. By the end of a year, you will be a seasoned baker who knows how to hit 2 per cent salt without scales.

This is the homeliest section of my book. Try my mum's delicious sourdough (see page 229-32) and enjoy using salt to improve your baking. A pinch of salt is the secret to success that's so often overlooked.

How it Works

When dissolved into a solution (normally water in bread making), salt's ions are forced apart by the solvent and break the geometric lattice that bonds the metal and acid together. This happens in a dough as the liquid dissolves salts into sodium, chloride and other ions.

Much of the science around salt and bread is very complex and still remains a bit of a puzzle to food scientists as to exactly how this works, but what is known is that when hydrated, glutens become *viscoelastic*, which means both viscous and elastic, and the dough can be stretched, released, flow over itself or retract back into an original shape. As you massage moisture into the wheat flour, the wheat's proteins create a network of gluten that can contain gases inside. Salt is key to this stretchy but impermeable matrix. The structure traps air bubbles and stops them floating outwards to escape. This trapped gas allows a bread to rise when the carbon dioxide produced by yeasts from fermentation is baked in and expands to form that aerated texture we know and love.

Beyond Flavour

It's only in the last couple of hundred years that we've all started incorporating salt into recipes, as prior to that it was so expensive. The primary role of salt is to enhance the flavour of bread. Adding in the region of 2 per cent salt to flour changes our perception of bread's flavour. It allows us to appreciate the full spectrum of taste, including the sweet notes. Without salt, bread is flat and insipid.

Carotenoid pigments from unbleached wheat flour are responsible for the creamy colour and rich aroma of bread. Salt is a natural antioxidant, so adding it to dough also delays oxidation of the carotenoids and preserves them in the mix for a fuller flavour. This is why salt is best added early in the process. As salt slows the rate of sugar consumption during fermentation, more residual sugar also becomes available when the salted dough is baked for a fuller, golden brown crust colouration. An indicator of unsalted bread will be its pale appearance and dull colour across the crust.

Unsalted vs Salted

Unsalted dough is bland, and although it mixes faster, it's very sticky and offers little resistance when kneading. As soon as salt is added, dough becomes tighter and stronger, capable of stretching without ripping. Interestingly, during fermentation, salt doughs rise more slowly, but there's a common misconception held by many home bakers that adding salt to bread may negatively impact on the bread rising by killing the yeasts or slowing them down. There is an element of truth there, but it's only a minor impact – only 10 per cent reduced functionality. In reality, the salt is busy strengthening and tightening the gluten proteins,

making it more resistant to the gas build-up from the yeast's fermentation – hence slower ferments in salted breads. The fact that salt retards the yeast's ability to ferment slightly is of minor consequence. You still need to be careful not to leave salt on yeasts in the bowl for any great length of time or it will kill them, but you can add both at the same time if you then mix well, as the salts will quickly dissolve into ions.

Which Salt to Use?

The answer really is that any salt will help chemically with bread making to build structure in wheat proteins and slow down fermentation. However, as a chef, I'm also searching for flavour, which is why I always choose to use artisan salts. Try to use fine sea salt flakes or milled Himalayan salt for a fine, even distribution and coverage to dissolve into a solution faster. Avoid moist crystals, coarse rock salt that's incredibly dense, or *sel gris* for breads, as their crunchy texture dissolves more slowly and won't be as helpful in doughs. Many chefs use kosher salt for baking because it's non-iodised and additive-free and this can be excellent as long as it contains more than just sodium chloride. The same theory applies to my breads as to all my other cooking – as a seasoned chef, you want to try to build flavour using minerally complex salts rather than refined, processed salt.

My Mum's Sourdough

I love baking at home but there's nothing more comforting than bread baked by your mum – so I've asked my mum, Brigit Strawbridge Howard, to share her sourdough recipe here in her own words....

Nothing makes a house feel more like a home than the smell of freshly baked bread; there's something wonderfully wholesome and nostalgic about the images it conjures up of childhood, family kitchens and bygone days. One of my own most vivid childhood memories is of my grandmother baking her weekly loaves. I can picture her as if it were only yesterday; hair pinned back in a bun at the nape of her neck, sleeves rolled up to her elbows, hands covered in flour, and dressed for 'business' in her cotton wrap-around pinny.

I'd watch, mesmerised, as my granny kneaded the soft white dough on her 1960s yellow formica table. The kneading process seemed to go on forever, and while she stretched and pummelled that dough, she would whistle along to tunes playing on the radio. Once kneaded, proved and knocked back, the dough would mostly be divided between four half-pound loaf tins (which I happily inherited, and still have today), but some would be kept back and formed into little round buns for us grandchildren when we came to stay. She made plaited loaves sometimes, too, and they were my favourites because I was allowed to help with the plaiting.

My sourdough journey began a few years back with the gift of a starter from James, harvested from his own robust and extremely active culture, known affectionately by my grandson, Indy, as 'Bubbly Mummy'. I've been through a number of bread-making phases in my own adult life, but until recently, I never once managed to recreate the taste and texture of my granny's loaves. However, since being inspired by James to have a go at making sourdough bread, I now bake regularly and cannot imagine ever buying bread from a shop again.

My first loaf was a disaster, as was my next, and the one after that. They were edible but my finished loaves looked more like pancakes. There are as many different recipes and instructions on how to make a sourdough loaf as there are varieties of flours you can use in it, but once you get the hang of the basic principles, you can play with the ingredients and timings and make the recipe your 'own'. I always use a rye starter, for instance, but other starters would doubtless work just as well. I also make a point of using the most wholesome ingredients I can find, preferring non-chlorinated water, organic flours made from ancient grains such as spelt, and Himalayan salt flakes, but these are not prerequisites, just preferences.

I ran out of salt, once. As I had already weighed out the other ingredients, I carried on, thinking it would be fine without. Big mistake! Without the salt to slow it down, the yeast ran wild overnight and when I came down in the morning, the dough had spilled over the edges of the bowl and begun to spread across the table. It was almost impossible to work with and I ended up with another 'pancake'. Worst still, the pancake tasted like cardboard.

Anyway, the recipe and method below is the one that always works best for me. I hope it works for you, too. And thank you, James, for including it in your book.

Makes 1 loaf/Serves 4

For activating the starter

Active rye sourdough starter
  (you can buy a starter from good
  bakeries, or find a recipe in James'
  book *The Artisan Kitchen*)
100g/3½oz tepid water
100g/3½oz light (white) rye flour

For the sourdough loaf

350g/12oz tepid water
2 tbsp agave syrup (or 3 tbsp sugar)
400g/14oz wholegrain spelt flour
140g/5oz white spelt flour, plus extra
  for dusting
10g/¼oz sea salt flakes
Rice flour, for sprinkling

Stage 1 – in advance of bake day

Day 1 morning:
Activate the starter. Remove the starter from the fridge and measure 50g/1¾oz of it into a large jar or glass bowl. Add 50g/1¾oz of the tepid water and 50g/1¾oz of the rye flour and mix together. Cover and leave for 24 hours at room temperature (around 21°C/70°F). I usually put mine on a sunny windowsill. By the time you to go bed, it should have doubled in size and be looking quite 'bubbly'.

Day 2 morning:
Discard half the starter. Add the remaining 50g/1¾oz of tepid water and the remaining 50g/1¾oz of rye flour to the active starter you have kept, mix together, then cover and leave again at room temperature for around 6 hours till late afternoon/early evening. You are now ready to start making your loaf.

Stage 2 – mixing the dough

Day 2 late afternoon/early evening:
For the sourdough loaf, put the tepid water, agave syrup (or sugar) and 75g/2¾oz of the activated starter into a large bowl (put the remaining activated starter back in the fridge). Mix together with a spoon or a hand whisk.

Add both spelt flours and the salt. Mix together to form a 'shaggy' dough. Mixing doesn't take more than a minute or two and I use a Danish dough whisk for this stage, but you could use a wooden spoon. Cover with a tea towel or polythene bag and leave to rest at room temperature for an hour.

After an hour, stretch and fold the dough ten times in the bowl. Cover again and leave to rest at room temperature for another hour. Do three more stretch and folds with 30 minutes rest between each. Cover the dough as before and leave overnight at room temperature.

Stage 3 – bake day

Day 3 morning:
The dough should have risen overnight. I pop mine in the fridge for an hour when I come down in the morning, to help firm it up before handling again.

Sprinkle a 22cm/8½in round (8.5cm/3¼in deep) proving basket or banneton with white spelt flour. If you don't have one of these you can use a glass mixing bowl.

Using a plastic scraper, first dip it in flour, then use to scrape the dough out of the bowl onto a floured surface. Bring the four edges of dough in on top of each other, turn over and shape into a boule. Keep shaping the boule till it's nice and tight (this part is really important to help stop it spreading in the oven).

Using a plastic scraper, scoop up the dough and tip it, top-side down, into the floured proving basket/banneton/bowl. Place the proving basket/banneton/bowl inside a large polythene food bag (or cover with a slightly damp tea towel) and leave to prove for 1–1½ hours, depending on the temperature of the kitchen.

Preheat the oven to 230°C fan/480°F/gas mark 9½ and preheat a baking tray. Use the 'steam' mode if you have it, otherwise add a shallow roasting tray filled with boiling water to the bottom of the oven.

Remove the hot baking tray from the oven and sprinkle with a liberal amount of rice flour (rice flour is brilliant because it doesn't burn at high temperatures like other flours).

Flip the dough onto the tray (if the dough is sticking to the basket/banneton/bowl, sprinkle a little rice flour around the edges to ease it out from the edges). Score a cross on the top of the boule with a sharp knife.

Bake for 15 minutes, then turn the oven down to 190°C fan/410°F/gas mark 6½ and bake for another 30 minutes or until dark brown and the loaf has a hollow sound when you knock the bottom of it. Transfer to a wire rack to cool completely, then serve in thick slices.

The loaf will keep fresh in a bread bin or sealed in a food storage bag for up to 7 days. Try toasted sourdough with cheese and chutney, smoked mackerel pâté (see recipe on page 87) or with a bowl of pumpkin soup.

Top Tips

Don't allow the dough to rise too much in the proving basket/banneton/bowl for its final prove before baking. If you do, it may not rise further in the oven.

Keep a small tub of the starter in the freezer, just in case yours expires. It reactivates surprisingly well! Defrost before use.

Discarded or leftover activated starter can be used to make other delicious goodies, such as crumpets (see recipe on page 240), muffins and crackers (see recipe on page 241).

Wild Garlic Focaccia

This recipe is fantastic for trying different seasonal ingredients as toppings
or adding another type of herby pesto, depending on what you have growing
in the garden. The brine poured over the bread before the final rise is
a superb way to season the focaccia. I have made lots of focaccia over
the years, mainly using large crunchy sea salt flakes to finish the bread.
However, nowadays, I prefer Samin Nosrat's Ligurian-style focaccia, where
a brine is poured over the dough before the final rise. It settles into the
dimples and edges, creating a golden, crunchy exterior with a steady wave of
seasoning rather than strong pops of salty flavour. Now, the olives or capers
have their moment to shine and deliver the salty bursts that I previously
used sea salt flakes for (though I do still sprinkle over a few salt flakes for
extra texture in my recipe below).

   Both methods work well, so it's completely your choice which way to
go. The key thing to take away is focaccia loves salt and, if done right, a
chunk of the infused bread with a bowl of nutty olive oil and some balsamic
vinegar to dip in on the side is more than enough for a rustic lunch.

For the focaccia
800g plain flour
600ml lukewarm water
4 tbsp olive oil
1 tbsp honey
½ tsp yeast
Pinch of sea salt flakes

For the wild garlic pesto
150ml extra virgin olive oil or rapeseed
   oil
150g or a large handful of wild garlic
   or nettle leaves
50g pine nuts or pumpkin seeds
50g grated parmesan
1 garlic cloves, finely chopped
Juice and zest of ½ lemon
Pinch of salt to taste

For the brine
1 tbsp water
1 tbsp olive oil
1 tsp sea salt

Make the focaccia dough. Whisk the warm water, yeast and honey
together in a jug, then leave for 5–10 minutes until bubbly. In a large
bowl, mix the flour and salt together to distribute the salt evenly.

   Combine the measured oil, the yeasty water and seasoned flour
together to make a dough. Stir the dough well, then scrape the sides
of the bowl with a plastic dough scraper to fold it over on itself. Form
into a smooth ball and cover with clingfilm or a damp tea towel. Leave
to ferment at a warm room temperature for 12 hours or until the dough
has doubled in size.

   Make the wild garlic pesto by blitzing all the ingredients (except the
salt) together in a food processor or using a large pestle and mortar
until smooth. Season to taste with the salt. Set aside to add to the
dough later. Keep the leftover pesto in a sealed jar in the fridge for
up to 1 week.

   Line a non-stick baking tray that is approx. 20 x 30cm/8 x 12in in size
with baking parchment and drizzle with a couple more tablespoons of
olive oil.

   Next, add 2 tablespoons of the pesto to the dough and carefully fold
through the dough – fold the dough over on itself in half one way from
the far side of the bowl towards you, then rotate 90° and fold again.
Turn and repeat for each of the four sides until the pesto is evenly

marbled (adding the pesto in this way knocks back the dough), then pour the dough out of the bowl onto the greased tray. Drizzle over a little more oil and then pull the dough out to the edges of the baking tray. Leave it covered, as before, somewhere warm, then after 30 minutes proving, repeat the stretching again as the dough will probably shrink back from the sides.

Make lots of small dimples in the top of the dough by pressing your fingers down into it. Now comes the fun bit of choosing how to spread out the toppings. Press these gently into the dough to half bury them.

Make the brine by whisking together the salt and water until the salt is dissolved, then pour this over the dough to fill the dimples. Cover with a tea towel and leave to prove in a warm place for a final 45 minutes–1 hour until the dough looks light and bubbly again.

While the bread is proving for the final time, preheat the oven to 220°C fan/475°F/gas mark 9.

Sprinkle the focaccia with a few more sea salt flakes. Bake for 30–35 minutes until golden brown on the top – check the bottom is also nice and crisp underneath.

Remove from the oven and brush the focaccia with a little more oil which will soak in as the bread begins to cool on the baking tray, then after 5 minutes, transfer to a wire rack to cool fully.

Cut and serve fresh or store the focaccia wrapped in baking parchment in an airtight bag to keep it moist for a few days.

Tear 'n' Share

Introducing my tear 'n' share bread – anarchy for the whole family. This salty bread is my ode to the mosh pit of my youth. When I was younger, I used to love a little chaos in the school holidays – dressed in torn, baggy jeans, band-worshipping in muddy festival fields. Reaching into the middle of the table and tearing a chunk of this cheesy bread takes me straight back to a time in my life when plates were optional. Have fun with this one while you are baking and whack on a record that reminds you of being young.

You can try the same recipe with caper berries and rosemary or replace the brie with a ball of burrata in the centre and dress it up with torn fresh basil. Go crazy and double up the centre-gap with a rich three-cheese sauce and treat it like a hedonistic twist on a fondue.

Makes 1 loaf/Serves 4–6

For the bread dough
7g/⅛oz dried active yeast granules
300ml/½ pint lukewarm water
500g/1lb 2oz strong white bread flour, plus extra for dusting
1 tsp sea salt flakes
Pinch of caster sugar
Olive oil, for oiling the bowl

For the tear 'n' share
1 whole brie or Camembert, about 250g/9oz
2 bulbs roasted garlic, with the tops sliced off
6–8 sprigs thyme
Milk, to glaze
1 tbsp panko breadcrumbs
1 tsp lemon and thyme sea salt flakes (available online, or make your own)

Line a baking tray with baking parchment and set aside.

Make the bread dough by whisking the yeast into the warm water in a jug and leaving it to ferment for 5–10 minutes.

In a large mixing bowl, combine the flour, salt and sugar. Add in the bubbly yeasty water and mix well to make a dough. Turn out the dough onto a floured surface and knead for 10–12 minutes.

Form into a ball and place in an oiled bowl. Cover with a damp tea towel and leave somewhere warm to rise for 1 hour until doubled in size.

For the tear 'n' share, knock the dough back and slice into 16 equal portions. Roll into balls and arrange in a diamond shape on the lined baking tray, leaving a gap in the middle. Place the whole cheese in the centre, then cut open the middle of the cheese to place a roasted garlic bulb in the centre. Squeeze out the garlic cloves from the second roasted bulb and stick them in the gaps between the dough balls. Stick sprigs of thyme in the gaps, too.

Brush with milk and sprinkle with the breadcrumbs. Finish with the lemon and thyme sea salt flakes. Cover with a tea towel or clingfilm and leave to prove somewhere warm for 45–50 minutes until roughly doubled in size.

Preheat the oven to 200°C fan/425°F/gas mark 7.

Bake the loaf for 10 minutes. Reduce the temperature to 180°C fan/400°F/gas mark 6 and continue to bake for another 20–25 minutes until the loaf has a golden crust with fluffy bread beneath. The cheese will have completely melted, too.

Serve warm and enjoy with friends or family. This bread can be stored in an airtight container in the fridge for 5–7 days and is best reheated before serving.

Pizza Dough

The key to a good pizza is the combination of baking a good dough in a really hot oven and then choosing toppings that excite you. I've made hundreds of different pizza toppings and have included a few of my favourites for inspiration here. Take time making the pizza dough and the rest will look after itself. Embrace seasonality and try an autumnal roasted squash, sage and chestnut pizza with blue cheese, or a wild garlic, new potato and smoked Cheddar pizza in the springtime.

Makes about 6–7 pizzas

For the pizza dough
600ml/1 pint lukewarm water
6g/⅛oz dried active yeast granules
1kg/2lb 4oz '00' flour, plus extra for
    dusting (or you can use semolina
    for rolling out the pizza dough)
10g/¼oz fine sea salt
1 tsp olive oil, for oiling the bowl

For the cockle pizza
(quantities given are per pizza)
2 tbsp tomato sauce
50g/1¾oz mozzarella, drained
    and sliced
Handful of cooked cockles
4 quarters of Preserved Lemon
    (see page 96), thinly sliced
½ tsp capers in brine or vinegar,
    drained
1 tsp chilli oil
1 tsp chopped flat-leaf parsley

For the goats' cheese pizza
2 tbsp caramelised onion chutney
50g/1¾oz mushrooms, sliced
1 tbsp The Full Works Sauce (see page 120)
1 tsp chopped rosemary leaves
4–5 slices *chèvre* (goats' cheese)
Pinch of cracked black pepper

For the pizza dough, get a large bowl and add the warm water and yeast. Whisk until the yeast is dissolved and bubbly. Add a couple of tablespoonfuls of the flour to make a batter-like consistency – it's best doing this with your hands or a dough whisk.

Gradually add the remaining flour and lastly the salt. Mix together to make a dough, then turn out onto a work surface. The dough will be a little tacky, so dust your hands in flour if you need to. Knead for around 20 minutes until the dough looks smooth and stretchy. Prod it with your finger, it should leave an indentation that slowly springs back. Put the dough into a clean bowl, cover with a damp tea towel and leave to rest in a warm place for 1 hour.

Turn the dough out of the bowl and gently knock out the air, then gently fold and shape it into a ball. Place the dough in a clean, oiled bowl, then cover with clingfilm or place in a sealed proving box if you have one. Leave the dough to ferment in the fridge for 48 hours.

On the day of baking, remove the dough from the fridge and shape into 6 or 7 balls, about 250g/9oz each. Place on a large baking sheet, cover with clingfilm or a tea towel and leave to rest at room temperature for around 4 hours. The dough will increase a little in size and smell amazing.

Gently stretch each ball of dough out on a floured (or semolina dusted) surface and form into a pizza shape. Slide each pizza, one at a time, onto a pizza peel and then add your chosen topping – you can also stretch the dough a little further, the weight of the topping will help.

For the toppings, spread the sauce/chutney onto the dough with the back of a ladle or large spoon. Make concentric circles and gently push it out from the middle to the edges.

When placing toppings on a pizza base, bear in mind that less is often more. Use good-quality mozzarella, seafood and fresh or roasted vegetables. Try adding robust herbs like rosemary and thyme before baking and delicate herbs such as basil, oregano or parsley once the pizza comes out of the oven.

For the tomato pizza

2 tbsp tomato sauce

50g/1¾oz mozzarella, drained
  and sliced

1 heritage tomato, thinly sliced

4 tsp spicy salsa verde

Pinch of sea salt

6–8 basil leaves, torn

Handful of rocket, to finish (optional)

Bake each pizza at 350°C/660°F in a wood-fired oven for 1–3 minutes and turn regularly with a smaller peel. If baking in a domestic oven, preheat the oven to 220°C fan/475°F/gas mark 9 and bake for 10–12 minutes, and use a pizza stone or salt block for extra radiated heat.

Once baked, finish the pizzas with a flavoured oil, a little cracked black pepper or a handful of rocket.

(*Top left*) *Cockle pizza*
(*Above*) *Goats' cheese pizza*
(*Left*) *Tomato pizza*

Sourdough Crumpets

This is another recipe from my mum's sourdough collection – homemade crumpets that use the sourdough starter which I gave to her a few years ago. It's called 'Bubbly Mummy' – named by my son, not me, I hasten to add. It's an easy recipe to make but I'd urge you to get crumpet rings if you want them to look authentic. The rings help provide some structure when they start cooking, otherwise they will sink and look more like pikelets.

Makes 6

250g/9oz active sourdough starter, fed (see page 230)

1 tbsp caster sugar

½ tsp sea salt

½ tsp bicarbonate of soda

Vegetable oil, for greasing

Unsalted butter, honey and sea salt flakes, to serve

Ideally, you'll need six 9cm/3½in crumpet rings.

Mix the sourdough starter with the sugar and salt in a bowl and stir in the bicarb.

Using kitchen paper, lightly rub a flat griddle and the crumpet rings with oil to grease. Preheat the seasoned griddle over a medium heat until it's hot, then place the crumpet rings onto the griddle.

Spoon the batter into the crumpet rings, leaving at least a 1cm/½in space in the top of each ring for the crumpets to rise without overflowing. Cook over a medium heat for 3–4 minutes until the crumpet batter is cooked and comes away from the edge of the rings.

Remove the crumpet rings and transfer the crumpets to a wire rack. Leave to cool, then eat the crumpets, buttered, with honey and a few sea salt flakes.

Gouda and Fenugreek Discard Crackers

It was about six or seven years ago that I was introduced to the combination of Gouda and fenugreek. My friend Giel and his family produce Cornish Gouda at their farm a few miles up the road from where I live. They produce a range of cheese including some excellent flavoured Gouda such as honey and clove, truffle and cumin. My personal favourite is, and always will be, the fenugreek Gouda. It is nutty, perfumed, aromatic, spicy and perfectly seasoned. The ideal ingredient to play with as a chef.

For this recipe, I wanted to show how sourdough discard can be given a complete facelift and transformed into the most delicious crackers. The discard is the excess flour, water and wild yeasts mix that normally goes to waste when feeding a sourdough starter at home. To me, it always seems like a dreadful waste, but it's the cost of keeping your starter culture healthy and bubbly, ready for bread making. This recipe gives the discard its own moment to shine. Perfect served with my Fermented Garlic Chutney (see page 133).

Makes 12 crackers

200g/7oz sourdough starter discard
  (see page 230)
2 tbsp finely grated Gouda cheese
1 tsp fenugreek seeds
½ tsp *fleur de sel*

Preheat the oven to 200°C fan/425°F/gas mark 7 and line a baking tray with baking parchment.

Using a palette knife, thinly spread the sourdough starter discard out on the lined baking tray, making sure it's even.

Sprinkle evenly with the grated Gouda and fenugreek seeds. Finish with the salt flakes.

Bake for 12–15 minutes until the edges start to crisp up. Allow to cool on the baking tray for a few minutes, then crack into shards, transfer to a wire rack to finish cooling and then serve warm or cold.

Once cooled, you can store the crackers in an airtight container for up to 2 weeks, but mine never last that long – we eat them straight off the tray with my garlic chutney or some hummus.

Carnitas Tacos

This recipe packs a heavyweight punch and is a contender for the title of my ultimate comfort food recipe. The seasoning is essential to success – a ferocious, dancing balance of smoked salt on the pork shoulder stuffed inside a soft flatbread.

Serves 8

For the smoky BBQ seasoning
1 tbsp smoked paprika
1 tbsp Smoked Sea Salt flakes
   (see page 216)
1 tsp fennel seeds
1 tsp dried ancho chilli flakes
1 tsp smoked garlic powder
1 tsp dried oregano
½ tsp cumin seeds

For the carnitas
2kg/4lb 8oz boned pork shoulder
   (in one piece)
2 tbsp Smoky BBQ Seasoning (above)
350ml/12fl oz IPA beer
2 tbsp cider vinegar
2 tbsp olive oil
4 garlic cloves, finely diced
2 tbsp chopped jalapeños
   (fresh or jarred)
2 tbsp light or dark soft brown sugar

For the flatbreads (Makes 8)
200g/7oz plain flour, plus extra
   for dusting
Pinch of fine sea salt flakes
100ml/3½fl oz room temperature water
1 tbsp olive oil
1 tbsp active sourdough starter (optional)
   (see page 230)

To serve and garnish
Guacamole
Frijoles
Pink pickled onions, drained
Lime quarters, for squeezing

Mix all the ingredients for the smoky BBQ seasoning together in a small bowl to ensure an even blend. Store any leftover seasoning (or if making a larger batch) in an airtight container after making this recipe (it is also great sprinkled on chicken or halloumi). This seasoning will keep in a sealed jar in the larder for up to 3 months.

For the carnitas, slice the pork shoulder into 6 large steaks and rub the BBQ seasoning into the meat all over. Leave the steaks on a wire rack (with a tray below) to marinate overnight in the fridge so they lightly dry cure and absorb the smoky flavours.

The next day, in a jug, whisk together the beer, vinegar, oil, garlic, jalapeños and brown sugar. Place the pork steaks in a shallow dish, pour over the wet marinade to cover the pork, then cover and leave to marinate in the fridge for a further 8–12 hours.

Preheat the oven to 160°C fan/350°F/gas mark 4.

Transfer the marinated pork steaks to a roasting tin and cover with foil, then roast for 5–6 hours until they are soft enough to pull apart with a spoon.

Meanwhile, make the flatbreads by whisking the flour and salt together in a small bowl. Pour the water into a larger bowl, then gradually whisk in the flour/salt mixture with a fork. Add the oil and the sourdough starter (if using – for extra flavour) halfway through mixing. Once the dough comes together, start kneading it on a floured work surface. Knead for 4–5 minutes, then cover with clingfilm or a tea towel and leave to rest at room temperature for 1 hour.

Divide the dough into 8 balls and roll out each one with a floured rolling pin into a 15cm/6in round or use a tortilla press.

Heat a non-stick frying pan or a seasoned cast-iron skillet over a high heat until hot. Cook the flatbreads, one at a time, over a high heat for 1–2 minutes on each side. Remove and keep loosely wrapped in a folded tea towel before serving to keep the flatbreads soft and warm.

Fill the flatbreads with guac, frijoles and the carnitas. Garnish with pink pickled onions, chopped coriander and finish with a squeeze of lime juice.

Chapter Seventeen
Plant-based

Salts are the architects of flavour. They map out taste with technical precision, drawing blueprints for how ingredients will react with the accuracy of a structural engineer. Understanding the schematics of salt and its relationship to sour, bitter, sweet and umami will enable you to build skyscrapers of flavour. If you are a vegetarian, learning more about salt is also essential to your diet. Salts rarely occur naturally in fruits or vegetables other than in things like samphire or seaweed.

I believe that if we are to eat a more sustainable plant-based diet, we first need to relearn the art of seasoning. Seasoning vegetables can be as sexy as sprinkling flakes of pure white salt over prawns grilling on the barbie. A chargrilled cauliflower steak can be as mouth-watering, if not more so, as a ribeye steak. Slices of grapefruit frankly look naughty when sprinkled with a white sequin salty dress.

Bittern

When salts are made in a crystallisation tank or salt ponds, there is a stage late in the evaporation process where the brine thickens into a mineral-rich soup of salts called *Bittern* or *Nigari*.

It is a sodium-depleted brine rich in magnesium, calcium and potassium ions and is used as a coagulant in the production of tofu – the bittern also preserves and enhances the natural flavours of the soy beans. There are many ways to make tofu using bittern derivatives (you can also make it with Epsom salt) and I have made it with nigari – magnesium chloride flakes – dissolved into my soy milk.

The Power of Veg

Vegetables have such immense flavour and salt amplifies them in a way that astounds me every time I cook. Veg can be salted, brined, cured, fermented and salt baked, but the best way to include more salt in a vegetarian diet, in my humble opinion, is to go back to the tomato test. Taste vegetables, both raw and cooked, with a table salt versus a good mineral-laced sea salt. All vegetables taste like the truest

form of themselves – if you season them well, they are outspoken and brave.

In this section, I've included a few plant-based recipes that I love and want to share with you. They all use salt to enhance but not to disguise. Let the other ingredients do the song writing. Let salt do the singing!

(Above) A simple pinch of salt to season these vegetarian faggots makes all the difference to bring out the roasted flavours. A wonderful contrast with sweet beetroot and umami mushroom and chestnut stuffing.

Umami Depth

I'm a seasonal-eating, local omnivore so I get a lot of umami tastes from cooking with meat, and fish and browning fats. I often think that vegan cookery is one of the more challenging ways to introduce umami but it's not impossible. Try using foods with more embodied salt like soy sauce, stock and seaweed flakes or dashi broth. Using more ingredients like porcini, truffles, caramelised onions and miso is another superb way to inject umami into a recipe.

Start by making your own seaweed salt (see recipe on page 277) and using it on nearly everything for a sublime, robust seasoning. I've even made a seaweed coffee tiramisu once and the seaweed was a game-changer. Take control and season your vegetables with flair. Vegetarian cookery is definitely the most exciting space for seasoning to revolutionise food.

Every day I harvest fresh veg, the sense of anticipation simmers away like a pot on the boil. For example, this afternoon I'm off to our family allotment to harvest the first peas of the year and tender sprouting broccoli. I'm going to make a minted seaweed salt to season them and serve them on a bed of gently spiced dal. The thought of that supper adventure fills me with an electric buzz.

How to Make Tofu

For me, tofu is a blank canvas waiting for a splash of colour. It's the perfect
vegan food to make an impact on and throw flavours at to create a dynamic
palate. Making your own tofu from scratch is surprisingly easy to have a go at,
but takes a little practice and artistry to master. It can then be cooked quickly
in stir-fries, or grilled or smoked to add buckets of flavour.

**Makes about 1 x 150g/5½oz
block of tofu**

350g/12oz dried organic soy
beans, washed

1 tbsp nigari flakes or magnesium
chloride (both available to buy online),
dissolved in 3 tbsp water

Soak the soy beans overnight in a large bowl of cold water.

Drain the beans, then blitz them with 2 litres/3½ pints of fresh water in
a food processor in batches to form a frothy bean milk.

Pour this bean milk into a large saucepan and bring the pulpy liquid to
the boil. Stir occasionally so it doesn't stick. Reduce the heat and simmer,
uncovered, for 15 minutes. Pour the mixture into a colander or sieve lined
with a piece of cheesecloth or muslin and leave to drain until it's cool
enough to handle, then squeeze the liquid out of the pulp or *okara*.

Pour just the soy milk back into a clean saucepan and heat until just
below boiling point (compost the *okara*). Remove from the heat and add
in the dissolved nigari flakes or magnesium chloride. Stir well and then
cover and leave for 10–15 minutes to allow curds to form.

Line a colander or sieve again with a fresh piece of cheesecloth or
muslin and gently pour in the curds. Leave to strain for 10–15 minutes.

Transfer the solid curds to a tofu mould or tofu press and press down
with a weight or by placing a couple of tins on top (if not using the tofu
press). Leave in the fridge for 12–24 hours to press out as much whey
as possible.

Unmould or remove the tofu from the mould or press (discard the
whey), then store in an airtight container in the fridge. Use within 2 weeks.

Smoked Tofu Katsu

If I'm given the choice between a marinated block of smoked tofu and plain tofu, it's an absolute no-brainer. The wood smoke flavour of tofu seasoned with soy sauce is turbo-charged with some serious fire power. If you want to bring out the big guns at a dinner party, smoked tofu with katsu sauce is a real crowd-pleaser. Lime juice shouldn't be underestimated when it's time to serve. A brief glance of bright acidity balances out the low tobacco clouds.

Serves 2

For the tofu

1 x 150g/5½oz block of Tofu
   (see page 247)
1 tbsp sesame oil, plus an extra splash
   for cooking
1 tbsp light soy sauce
1 tsp mirin
Handful of hickory sawdust or fine
   shavings

For the katsu sauce

1 carrot, peeled and finely diced
1 onion, finely diced
6 garlic cloves, finely diced
2 tbsp sesame oil
1 tbsp mild curry powder
2 tbsp plain flour
700ml/1¼ pints vegetable stock
1 tbsp dark soy sauce, or to taste
2 tsp runny honey
Sea salt and cracked black pepper

To serve

4–6 spring onions, trimmed and
   left whole
Pinch of shichimi togarashi
   (a Japanese seven-spice blend)
2 lime wedges

Marinade the tofu in the sesame oil, soy sauce and mirin in a dish at room temperature for 1–2 hours. Prepare the cold smoker by adding the hickory sawdust or fine shavings and lighting it about 10–15 minutes before you start, to generate smoke. Place the tofu onto the smoking rack and cold smoke for 6–8 hours, then remove from the smoker.

Towards the end of the smoking time, make the katsu sauce by sautéing the carrot, onion and garlic in the sesame oil in a frying pan over a medium heat. After 5 minutes, stir in the curry powder, then the flour, little by little. Cook out the flour for 1–2 minutes, then gradually stir in the stock.

Bring to the boil, then simmer for 15–20 minutes until thickened and browned. Blitz with a stick blender or in a food processor until smooth. Add the soy sauce and honey and season to balance the taste, adding extra soy sauce if required.

About 10 minutes before serving, char the spring onions in a hot ridged skillet over a high heat for about 6–7 minutes, turning regularly, then season with the shichimi togarashi. Just before serving, place the lime wedges, cut-side down, into the skillet alongside the spring onions and leave to caramelise for 2–3 minutes.

At the same time, heat a splash of sesame oil in a non-stick frying pan over a medium heat, add in the block of smoked tofu and cook for 4–5 minutes, turning once, until golden and starting to turn crispy on the edges.

Slice and serve the fried tofu on top of the katsu sauce and garnish with the charred spring onions, a pinch of shichimi togarashi and lime wedges.

Plant Burger

My plant burger is all about combining colour, texture and aroma to serve up a salivatingly tasty feast. Smoked sea salt in the jackfruit unlocks depth in the spices and other component parts which radically adds layers to the burger's flavour.

Makes 2

For the patties

200g/7oz (drained weight) tinned
   jackfruit, drained
100g/3½oz (drained weight) cooked
   or tinned chickpeas, drained
½ onion, finely diced
1 garlic clove, finely diced
1 tbsp gram flour, plus extra for
   shaping patties
2 tsp Cajun spice blend
½ tsp Smoked Sea Salt (see page 216)
55g/2oz panko breadcrumbs
Vegetable oil, for frying

For the pulled jackfruit

200g/7oz (drained weight) tinned
   jackfruit, drained
1 tbsp Cajun spice blend
Pinch of Smoked Sea Salt (see page 216),
   plus extra to finish
1 tbsp olive oil
85g/3oz barbecue sauce
2 tbsp crispy onions

To build the burgers

2 bread rolls, split in half
Spiced vegan mayo or burger relish
Salad leaves
1 ripe avocado, stoned, flesh scooped
   out and smashed
1 spring onion, finely sliced
Handful of jarred jalapeños, drained
   and sliced (optional)

Make the patties first by blitzing the jackfruit, chickpeas, onion, garlic, gram flour, Cajun spice blend and smoked salt in a food processor until you have a coarse mince texture.

Use a little extra gram flour to flour your hands, then form the mixture into two large patties and roll each one in the panko breadcrumbs to coat. Place in the fridge to chill while you prepare all the other ingredients.

For the pulled jackfruit, slice the jackfruit flesh, then toss with the Cajun spice blend and smoked sea salt in a bowl.

Heat the olive oil in a frying pan, add the jackfruit mixture and sauté over a medium heat for 4–5 minutes until it's starting to brown, then add the barbecue sauce. Reduce the heat and cover the pan. Cook for 15–20 minutes until it is soft and sticky, stirring occasionally. Once it's ready, use two forks to shred the jackfruit into a finer pulled texture. Season with a little more smoked sea salt to taste and add the crispy onions to finish.

Fry the burger patties in a little vegetable oil in a frying pan over a medium-high heat for about 5–6 minutes on each side until golden and firm on the outside.

Build the burgers in the rolls with some spiced mayo or burger relish on the base, then salad leaves, followed by a burger, then a decent handful of pulled jackfruit on top. Finish with the smashed avocado, spring onion and jalapeños.

Buffalo Cauliflower Wings

The key salt craft process here is pre-salting or brining the cauli before it's cooked. Brining vegetables helps to tenderise them, making them perfect for grilling and roasting. When you treat dense vegetables more like meat, you can really improve your cooking results on a grill. Very often, dense vegetables will burn before they soften – things like carrots, beetroots or sweet potatoes are notorious for charring on the outside but remaining hard and crunchy at the core.

Brining the cauliflower kickstarts the cooking process and you have a couple of options on how to do it. Either pre-salt the vegetables in a cold brine for 24 hours in advance or cook them in the brine to parboil before grilling. If time allows, I always choose to pre-salt the veg for 24–48 hours, as this also starts a mild fermentation which can slightly enhance the lactic-tang flavours, but either method works well. If you are cooking in the brine, then try to soak the vegetables in the water for at least 1–2 hours beforehand, so that some diffusion can start to take place. Seasoning the veg from within is the other key benefit of using a brine instead of simply sprinkling the outside with salt and relying on surface osmosis.

Serves 2

For the brined cauliflower

1 medium cauliflower, broken into florets
  (leaves and core discarded)

4 per cent sea salt to water (I use
  sel gris for this recipe) – see method

1 tbsp cider vinegar

1 tsp caster sugar

1 bay leaf

1 tsp black peppercorns

1 tsp dried chilli flakes

2 tbsp rapeseed oil

Pinch of chilli salt flakes or barbecue salt

To serve

4 tbsp hot pepper sauce

2 tbsp blue cheese dressing (optional)

Pinch or two of *sel gris* (or another
  crunchy crystal salt)

2 spring onions, finely sliced

½ green chilli, de-seeded and thinly
  sliced (optional)

4 celery sticks

Put the cauli florets into a saucepan. Measure/weigh how much water it takes to cover the cauliflower florets in the pan and then add 4 per cent of this weight (of the water) in salt to the water (so if you are using 500ml/18fl oz of water, you'll need to add 20g/¾oz of salt). Add the vinegar, sugar, bay and spices. Stir well to dissolve the salt. Cover the pan and leave for as much time as you have available, ideally 4–6 hours. The longer you pre-salt the cauli florets for, the more tender they will be when you grill them.

Next, I like to parboil the cauliflower in the brine for 5–10 minutes. Once parboiled, strain the cauli florets in a colander and leave to dry for a few minutes to allow some water to evaporate off, then tip into a bowl and toss with the rapeseed oil and chilli or barbecue salt.

Grill the cauli florets (in a single layer) on a rack over a hot barbecue or on a baking parchment-lined baking tray under a preheated hot grill, for 10–15 minutes, turning occasionally, until they start to char.

Once ready, toss the florets in the hot pepper sauce and serve with a drizzle of blue cheese dressing (if using) and a pinch or two of *sel gris* (or another crunchy crystal salt) to season. Garnish with the spring onions and green chilli (if using), with the celery sticks served on the side.

Salty Salad Spray

This salty salad spray gently coats each leaf and vegetable with a light touch of salt but nothing else. I adore the simplicity of using a liquid salt to season a salad rather than relying on heavy oils and acidic vinegar. The flavours you get to taste are so clean and simple. Stripped back, pure and honest. For me, this is as basic as cooking gets but there are a few hidden reasons why it works so well. Firstly, choose a great selection of tasty seasonal ingredients, cut differently; grated, sliced, peeled or diced. Include some toasted seeds or nuts for extra crunch. Toss all the ingredients well while spraying for an even chiffon-thin layer of shimmering spray to fall gracefully onto the leaves.

The word salad comes from the Roman habit of salting bitter leaves before eating them and it's astounding how, with a little salt, a bowl of even the most bitter greens can become infinitely more palatable.

Serves 4

For the salty spray
25g/1oz sea salt

For the chopped salad
4–6 sprouting broccoli stems, steamed and cooled, left whole
2 asparagus spears, steamed, cooled and thinly sliced
1 large Salad Bowl lettuce or iceberg lettuce, roughly chopped
250g/9oz (drained weight) tinned mixed beans, drained
1 carrot, peeled and then shaved into ribbons with a peeler
1 celery stick, sliced
1 red onion, sliced
½ fennel bulb, finely sliced
Handful of sprouted seeds
2 tbsp toasted seeds, such as sunflower, pumpkin or hemp seeds
1 tbsp capers in brine or vinegar, drained

For the salty spray, dissolve the salt in 100ml/3½fl oz of water in a jug, then transfer to a small, clean spray bottle.

For the chopped salad, prepare all the ingredients and gently toss to mix in a large bowl.

Season the salad with the salty spray after every couple of turns for an even dynamic of salty back notes. Alternatively, leave the salad naked and place the salt spray on the table for your guests to season themselves.

Store the leftover salt spray in the fridge and use within 1 week.

Salt Geek

Try cucumber, lemon or fresh Mediterranean herbs infused in the salty spray. This is also a great way to draw flavour from waste food products. Leave the cucumber peel, lemon rind or herb stalks to infuse the water for 24 hours at room temperature, then strain and dissolve the salt in the mildly aromatic flavoured water. Store flavoured salt sprays in the fridge in their spray bottles for up to 1 week.

Chapter Eighteen
Sweet and Salty

It's 7am and I'm taking bites from a bar of smooth dark chocolate with Himalayan salt – solely in the name of research, of course. This combination of sweet and salty is addictive and leaves me craving more. Scientifically, there is a convincing argument that says biological determinism is responsible for our cravings rather than just some greedy chocoholic's desire. Therefore, he says, taking another bite of salted chocolate from the bar on his desk, it is evolution that I must thank and blame for my cravings, not my own weak will.

How Does it Work?

When you eat food that is sweet and salty, two cravings are simultaneously satisfied. Recent research has shown that some sweet taste cells in our taste buds, the tiny sugar receptors on our tongue called SGLT1, only transport the message of sugars to the brain when sodium is present. Sweetness is accentuated when tasted with a little salt. Sugar is an energy source and salt is crucial to survival. We are pre-programmed to crave both sweet and salty flavours by the primal instincts that are still buried within our bodies.

We were designed to recognise sugar as an easy energy source with high calories and take it when we can find it; sugar-rich fruits would have been a lifeline for hungry hunter-gatherers when other food was scarce. Not only does sugar help us survive, it also releases dopamine when detected on the tongue, a complicated neurotransmitter that literally conveys happiness to the brain and makes us crave more. Furthermore, an underlying desire for variety would have been crucial for survival for our ancestors and perhaps this is why the combination of salt and sugar is so enthralling – it keeps us seeking a diverse mix of foods.

Alchemy

As contradictory as it sounds, a salty slice of air-dried ham wrapped around a wedge of watermelon makes the fruit taste sweeter. Chocolate-covered pretzels, sweet and salty popcorn, peanut butter and jelly are testament to this marriage of tastes which work together in harmony. Using salt carefully can help reduce the overpowering sweetness in certain sickly desserts by providing a balanced contrast and it also sharpens other more subtle flavours. At the same time, sugar softens the taste of a salty dish and rounds it off. You can achieve fantastic balance when the two tastes are correctly combined. Scandinavian-style soft cures often use sugar to soften the mix. The sugar actively alleviates harsh bitterness from mineral-rich sea salts.

Both sugar and salt are necessary minerals that improve brain function and lower stress. The danger is eating too much of a good thing – learn to control your cravings, but cut yourself some slack, as layering flavours helps make you a better cook and a happier human. The winning formula for the alchemy of taste lies in managing these sensory-specific tastes so that they are finely aligned and perfectly balanced.

(Opposite left) Salt caramel, (Above) Popcorn

Salted Caramel Sauce

We have pastry chefs and chocolatiers to thank for the salt caramel craze that started nearly fifteen years ago and still shows no sign of slowing down. Salt accentuates sweet flavours. A small dash of salt brings out the caramelised toffee notes in brown sugar. To me, it also makes cacao and chocolate taste richer, less bitter and more balanced.

Makes a 500g/1lb 2oz jar

175g/6oz light soft brown sugar
250ml/9fl oz double cream
55g/2oz unsalted butter, diced
1 tsp sea salt flakes

Tip the sugar into a heavy-based saucepan. Stir in 2 tablespoons of water and heat over a medium heat until dissolved.

Turn up the heat and cook for 4–5 minutes until you have a brown caramel (it should have reached around 121°C/250°F).

Take off the heat and stir in the cream and butter until combined. Stir in the salt.

Serve warm, or leave the sauce to cool, then store in a sealed jar or an airtight container in the fridge. Unopened, it will keep in the fridge for up to 1 month. Once opened, keep refrigerated and use within 1 week. It is best reheated gently in a pan to serve warm.

This sauce is delicious served with ice cream, drizzled over a baked cheesecake or used as an ingredient in desserts.

Salt Chocolate Truffles with Gorse

Silver birch is my favourite tree and gorse is my favourite flower. Both are leagues ahead of any rivals. There's a saying down here in Cornwall that kissing is only out of fashion when the gorse is not in bloom – because gorse flowers almost all year long. It's prolific, fragrant, bright and wild, and I think gorse smells like sweet coconut and cut grass mixed with honey. When the wind blows on a warm day, the exotic aroma rides vanilla skies as the gusts rise over the coastal paths, forcing you to close your eyes and breathe in the perfume surprise. It's the closest I will ever come to Caribbean island-living.

Makes about 24

For the truffles

225g/8oz 70 per cent dark chocolate,
  roughly chopped

50g/1¾oz double cream

200g/7oz Salted Caramel Sauce
  (see page 259)

To coat

2–3 tbsp cocoa powder

1 tbsp finely sliced gorse flowers

1 tsp sea salt flakes

150g/5½oz 70 per cent dark chocolate,
  roughly chopped

Make the truffle mixture. Over a bain-marie, melt the chocolate, then stir in the double cream. Remove from the bain-marie when it looks velvety and gently stir in the salted caramel sauce, but only stir until the mixture is smooth and glossy (if you stir it too much, it may separate), then put it straight in the fridge to chill.

After 2–3 hours of chilling, the truffle mix should be firm enough to shape into balls. Use a teaspoon to scoop out the truffle mix and form into small, similar-sized balls (each slightly smaller than a walnut – you'll make about 24). Place on a plate and return to the fridge for 30 minutes to set solid.

For the coating, mix the cocoa powder, gorse flowers and sea salt, then spread out on a marble block or a baking parchment-lined baking tray. Melt the chocolate over a bain-marie.

Dip the truffles into the melted chocolate and then immediately roll in the salty, gorse-flowered cocoa to coat. Leave to set.

Store in an airtight container in the fridge and try not to eat all of them at once. I'm lucky if a batch lasts a week in our house.

Smoked Salt Caramel Pumpkin Pie

If you want to talk about transatlantic recipe exchange, then this dish is a real success story. Every autumn in our household we bake pumpkin pie and it still surprises me how much my family has taken it to heart as a new food tradition. Perhaps it's the American side of my children's heritage that has predisposed them to love a slice of sweet pie, or maybe it's the British obsession with pastry. My version fuses my love of sweet and salty with a hint of smoke for added depth of flavour. I think that pumpkin spice always works well when it's heavily seasoned. It brings out the hearty, warming spice flavours and could also be used as a seasoning blend with a rustic apple cobbler, slow-roasted pork shoulder, gravlax with sage and whiskey or used to cure a spiced duck bresaola.

Makes one 22cm/8½in pie; Serves 6–8

Unsalted butter, for greasing

500g/1lb 2oz peeled and de-seeded pumpkin or squash flesh, diced

400g/14oz chilled homemade or shop-bought sweet shortcrust pastry

Plain flour, for dusting

2 eggs, plus 1 extra egg yolk, beaten

250ml/9fl oz double cream

70g/2½oz dark soft brown sugar, smoked as you would smoke salt (see page 216) if you want to turbo-charge the recipe

55g/2oz Salted Caramel Sauce (see page 259)

½ tsp Smoked Sea Salt (see page 216)

1 tsp ground cinnamon

½ tsp grated nutmeg

½ tsp ground ginger

Pinch of ground allspice or ground cloves

1 bay leaf (optional)

Sea salt flakes and salted caramel ice cream, to serve

Preheat the oven to 180°C fan/400°F/gas mark 6. Grease a 22cm/8½in round pie dish with butter and line the base with baking parchment.

Cook the pumpkin or squash in a pan of lightly salted boiling water for 20–25 minutes until soft enough to mash. Drain and leave to cool in a colander or fine sieve to reduce the water content of the purée and intensify the pumpkin/squash flavour.

Meanwhile, roll out the pastry on a lightly floured surface, then press into the prepared pie dish. Trim off the pastry to neaten and then blind-bake with baking parchment and baking beans for 15 minutes until pale golden in colour. Remove the baking beans and paper and return to the oven for another 5 minutes, then take out of the oven and set to one side.

Blitz the cooled pumpkin/squash in a food processor until smooth. Transfer to a fine sieve again and leave for a few more minutes to drain off the excess water.

Tip the pumpkin purée into a bowl and mix with the eggs and yolk, the cream, sugar, salted caramel sauce, smoked salt and ground/grated spices. Pour into the pastry case. Place a bay leaf in the centre to infuse with an extra aromatic flavour, if you like.

Bake for 45 minutes until the surface appears set with only a slight wobble – test with a skewer, it should come out clean rather than sticky. Remove from the oven, then leave to cool and set further.

Cut the pie into slices (remove the bay leaf when serving) and serve with a sprinkle of sea salt flakes and some salted caramel ice cream on the side.

Store any leftover pie in an airtight container in the fridge and eat within 5 days.

How to Ferment Apples

Fermented apples taste tangy and sharp like a medium-dry cider. They have a heady floral bouquet and I've also slightly spiced the apples for a mosh pit of flavour.

Serves about 4

4 Bramley apples, peeled, cored and
   roughly chopped

Fine sea salt flakes – you need 3 per
   cent weight of the prepped apples

1 tbsp runny honey

2 cinnamon sticks

Weigh the prepared apples, then calculate 3 per cent of this weight – this is how much salt you will need. Make a brine using the measured salt mixed with water. You will need approximately 1 litre/1¾ pints of water to cover the apples in a jar while they ferment (but it depends on how finely/roughly you chop them). If you need to top up with more water/brine, then make sure it is a 3 per cent brine.

Place the apples, honey and cinnamon sticks in a large, sterilised jar, then pour in the brine and make sure the apples and cinnamon sticks are covered by the liquid – keep them submerged with a fermentation weight placed on top so they don't float. Cover loosely with a lid to allow gases to escape.

Leave the apples to ferment for 7–10 days at room temperature (between 18–22°C/64–72°F) – by this time the apples have finished fizzing and fermentation slows down. Longer fermentation times will develop the best sour apple flavour.

Either use the apples immediately or tighten the lid and store in a cool, dark place for up to 3 months. Apples are lively when fermenting and the natural yeasts on the apples may also start to develop alcohol and turn to cider or vinegar, so I suggest releasing the gases every few days (by undoing, then re-tightening the lid) for the first 2–3 weeks of storage.

Fermented apples are delicious when drained from the brine and used with all sorts of pork recipes, in sausage rolls or stuffing, with grilled scallops and black pudding, or caramelised for a sour, sweet and tangy tarte Tatin.

Salt-fermented Apple Crumble

My son's favourite dessert is his mummy's apple crumble! This means that traditional apple crumble recipes are off the table at home for me, but if it's a crumble with a twist, then I'm not treading on any toes. So, I've radically punk-rocked this classic with my own baggy-jeaned 90s vibe by using fermented apples. The apples are a little less sweet than raw apples, so add a good dollop of salted caramel sauce to the filling as it cooks to bring back that sweet balance.

Makes one large family-sized crumble;
Serves 6

For the filling
1 x quantity Fermented Apples
   (see opposite)
50g/1¾oz unsalted butter
50g/1¾oz golden caster sugar
2–4 tbsp Salted Caramel Sauce
   (see page 259), to taste
1 tsp ground cinnamon
1 tsp ground ginger
½ tsp grated nutmeg

For the crumble topping
250g/9oz plain flour
150g/5½oz unsalted butter, diced
85g/3oz walnuts, finely chopped
100g/3½oz demerara sugar, plus
   extra to sprinkle on top
85g/3oz granola

Clotted cream, custard or vanilla ice
   cream, to serve

Preheat the oven to 180°C fan/400°F/gas mark 6.

For the filling, drain the brine from the fermented apples. Melt the butter in a saucepan over a low heat, then stir in the sugar, salted caramel sauce and spices and stir until the sugar is dissolved and combined.

Add the fermented apples to the pan and stir to mix, then transfer to a large (25cm/10in) pie dish.

Blitz all the crumble topping ingredients in a food processor or rub together by hand in a large bowl to form a nutty, coarsely-textured crumb. Arrange in a thick layer on top of the apple filling. Finish with a sprinkle of demerara sugar.

Bake for 20–25 minutes until golden and starting to bubble up from under the crumble. Serve warm with clotted cream, custard or vanilla ice cream.

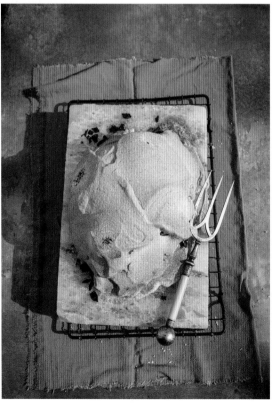

Salt-baked Pears with Miso Caramel

David Chang's *Lucky Peach* magazine was years ahead of its time. I reckon I could still look through my archive today and find pages with mind-blowingly innovative food ideas and trends that are yet to make it into the mainstream. I vividly remember the first time I read about burnt miso being used by a pastry chef in a banana pie that affectionately became known as Crack Pie. I had to try it for myself and ever since, I've been hooked! Liberally adding a spoonful of miso to my caramel is ridiculously tasty and moreish. This recipe comes with a health warning – miso caramel can be highly addictive, so consume responsibly!

Serves 4

For the salt crust

4 egg whites

115g/4oz fine Himalayan salt

50g/1¾oz caster sugar

2 cinnamon sticks

6 star anise

1 tbsp dried rose petals

1 Himalayan salt block, about
   30 x 20 x 4cm/12 x 8 x 1½in (optional)

4 whole unpeeled pears (ripe ones
   are best)

For the miso caramel

1 tbsp white miso paste, or to taste

85g/3oz Salted Caramel Sauce
   (see page 259)

To serve

Double cream

About 2 tbsp granola

Sprig fennel

A few edible flowers, such as
   fennel, daisies or borage (optional)

Preheat the oven to 180°C fan/400°F/gas mark 6.

For the salt crust, whisk the egg whites in a bowl until they form stiff peaks. Fold in the salt and sugar.

Arrange the cinnamon sticks, star anise and rose petals as a trivet on the salt block (if using) or on a baking tray and carefully arrange the pears on top. This aromatic bed will infuse the pears with loads of flavour while they bake.

Using a spatula, spread the salty meringue mixture over the pears so they're completely covered. Bake for 45–50 minutes until the salt crust turns brown and feels hard to tap.

While the pears are baking, make the miso caramel. Mix the miso paste with the salted caramel sauce in a small saucepan and warm through gently. Adjust the seasoning to taste with extra miso, if required. Keep warm.

When the salt-baked pears are ready, crack open the crust and lightly brush the pears clean. Slice the pears into segments and serve each portion with some double cream, a sprinkle of granola and the miso caramel drizzled on top. Decorate each portion with a small fennel frond and a couple or so edible flowers, if you have them.

Carrot and Gingerbread Slice with Salted Caramel

A salty gingerbread slice with treacle and caramel – absolute feel-good, decadent comfort food. I created this recipe to be a tribute to a carrot cake dessert I had years ago at Simon Rogan's Michelin-starred restaurant L'Enclume. Mine isn't at all sophisticated, but it delivers exactly what I remember salivating over. The killer combo of carrot and ginger finished with a sweet and salty flash of flavour that makes the squidgy pudding dirty, in a good way.

Makes 12 slices

For the gingerbread

150g/5½oz unsalted butter, plus
    extra for greasing
125g/4½oz dark muscovado sugar
150g/5½oz black treacle
200g/7oz golden syrup
1 tsp ground ginger
1 tsp ground cinnamon
1 tsp bicarbonate of soda
2 eggs, beaten
250ml/9fl oz whole milk
Good pinch of fine sea salt flakes
315g/11oz plain flour
2 medium carrots, peeled and grated

For the icing and to finish

150g/5½oz icing sugar, sifted
2 tbsp lemon juice
2 tbsp Salted Caramel Sauce (see
    page 259)
½ tsp salt pearls

Preheat the oven to 180°C fan/400°F/gas mark 6. Grease a baking tin (use one about 20 x 30cm/8 x 12in) with butter and line with baking parchment.

For the gingerbread, melt the butter, sugar, treacle, syrup, ginger and cinnamon together in a saucepan over a low heat until all the ingredients are fully combined, stirring regularly.

Remove from the heat and stir in the bicarb. Stir in the beaten eggs and milk. Now add a good pinch of salt to the mix and then pour the mixture into a large bowl. Add the flour and grated carrot and stir well so there are no big lumps.

Pour into the prepared tin, then bake for 35–40 minutes or until dark in colour and a skewer inserted in to the centre comes out clean. Cool the gingerbread slightly in the tin, then turn out onto a wire rack and leave to cool completely before decorating.

For the icing, mix the icing sugar with the lemon juice in a small bowl until it can be drizzled. Using a spoon, drizzle the gingerbread first with the lemon icing and then with the salted caramel sauce. Finish with the salt pearls sprinkled over. Cut into generous slices to serve and enjoy as a snack or dessert.

Keep any leftovers in an airtight container at room temperature for up to 10 days.

Chapter Nineteen
Drinks

For the sake of transparency, I think that it is worth confessing my passion for salty drinks of all kinds. I often drink bottles of fruity isotonic mixes when exercising in the belief that it will make me run faster and recover more quickly. I also love a cheeky tequila slammer on a big night out. To confess all my salty sins, I even once filled an entire paddling pool with margarita and edged the rim with sea salt. Having exposed my darkest salted secrets, I think it's now time to talk about why salty drinks rock my world.

Isotonics and Electrolytes

Sodium is the most important electrolyte; it helps you retain fluid and prevents dehydration. The more sweat you lose while exercising, the more you'll be at risk of dehydration or cramps. So it is important to replace these lost salts if undertaking intense exercise. There are lots of sports drinks out there that promise to replace electrolytes lost from sweating when exercising. But what does isotonic really mean and how can you learn to make your own drinks at home?

The concentration of isotonic drinks is allegedly designed to have a similar level of carbohydrates, sugar and salts as in our blood. Not only do these drinks replace lost salts, but they also boost our carb levels, so providing energy.

We need water, sodium and calories in different proportions to keep exercising for prolonged periods because they need to be replaced regularly. The most famous commercial drinks originally focused on sugar and some negligible salts. Gradually they've moved away from being solely fruity flavoured sugary drinks to refocus increasingly on electrolytes for athletes. The drinks evolved to cover a complex range of salts – primarily sodium, but also potassium, calcium and magnesium.

Many drinks will market the number of electrolytes they include, but the reality is still that the exact levels of calorie, water and electrolyte requirements are not the same for everyone. There's no one-size-fits-all product or brand. From person to person, we lose sweat at a different rate. Sodium loss can vary dramatically in sweat. To truly tailor hydration and electrolyte replacement, it would be worth taking a sweat test to see how much sodium you lose in your sweat. The future for salty drinks will be personalised drinks tailored to your body's needs!

There is also a key distinction between isotonic and hypotonic drinks. If you require rapid water absorption, hypotonic sports drinks contain lower levels of carbohydrate at around 3 per cent (rather than 6 per cent in isotonic drinks) and a much higher electrolyte content. More water in a hypotonic drink makes them better for endurance events and longer runs to reduce dehydration or cramp.

Salinity in Cocktails

Salt on the rim of a glass works fantastically to enhance a beverage, but if we look at what we've learned so far about salt, we also know that it enhances other liquids just as well, if not better, than food.

Salts, by their nature, work incredibly well in tandem with sugar. They make citrus taste brighter, enhancing the perception of sourness, although too much salt suppresses the acidity in citrus and other sharp ingredients. Mute bitterness with a pinch of salt and radically change the balance of flavour.

Mixologists and bartenders are making seasoned syrups and are starting to add salt to enhance their creations – like adding a few drops of bitters to round off the edges. If you want to play at home, try making a brine that is 1 part salt to 10 parts water and, using an old-fashioned dropper, add 1–2 drops to citrus-centred cocktails and up to as much as 10 drops into bitters.

Isotea

Timing is very important with isotonic drinks. Drinking small sips of a homemade isotea before feeling thirsty is a better way to rehydrate and provide yourself with some additional energy when working out. If you are already very thirsty, the chances are you've left it a little late. I've used my own homemade isotonic drinks with a tea base – hence isotea – for some time now while rowing and playing tennis and I really enjoy making and tailoring them to my own tastes. I tend to sweat quite heavily when I work out hard and have previously suffered from muscle cramps. I would say that since becoming more aware about salts with my cookery and incorporating them into my diet, it's now extremely rare for me to feel that I need to replenish with high levels of electrolytes. I see an isotea as a kind of top up or power pack that maintains a fully charged battery.

**Makes a 1 litre/1¾ pint bottle;
Serves about 2**

350ml/12fl oz cold-brewed green
tea or Earl Grey (I like a little caffeine
in my drinks – tea has roughly 50 per
cent compared to a cup of coffee)
140g/5oz fresh blueberries
1 tbsp lemon juice
2 tsp maple syrup or 30g/1oz golden
caster sugar
0.5g/good pinch of Persian Blue
rock salt, grated

Cold brew the tea the night before and keep it in the fridge, then strain and measure out the 350ml/12fl oz needed for this recipe.

Blitz the blueberries in a food processor with the strained tea, the lemon juice and maple syrup or sugar. Dilute with water to make up to 1 litre/1¾ pints of isotea. Add in the grated salt and taste to adjust the acidity or sweetness to suit your preference, but try to remain within these measurements for an effective drink to take when working out for 1–2 hours. This quantity of Isotea should deliver enough sugar and salt to last two training sessions.

Pour into a clean bottle(s), screw the lid(s) on and store in the fridge for up to 3 days.

Top Tips

*Try adding freshly squeezed
orange juice instead of tea
for an isotonic drink that's
higher in sugars for high-
energy, short workouts and
that includes maltodextrin
– this is a water-soluble type
of carbohydrate that provides
extra fuel for intense exercise.*

Salty Dog

Use a good-quality gin or vodka for this cocktail as the ingredients are so simple there is nowhere to hide.

Makes 1 cocktail

1 egg white, beaten (optional)

2 tbsp fine Himalayan salt or fine sea salt flakes

Ice, to serve

Double shot (50ml/2fl oz) gin or vodka

3 shots (75ml/2½fl oz) grapefruit juice, freshly squeezed (I prefer to use pink grapefruit, but any type will do)

A little samphire, to garnish

Either dampen the rim of the cocktail glass in water or dip in the beaten egg white on a saucer to make the rim sticky. Tip the Himalayan salt or fine salt flakes onto a small tray, then gently roll the rim of the glass in the salt.

Add some ice to the glass. Pour the gin or vodka and grapefruit juice over the rocks and garnish with a little samphire. Enjoy!

Bloody Mary

If you have ever ordered a Bloody Mary on an aeroplane perhaps you will have experienced a craving for salt and umami flavours that's almost instantly satisfied. When we fly at altitude, we lose up to 30 per cent of our ability to taste. Food and drink become extremely bland, so either umami-rich options are chosen for the menu or salt is added to intensify our ability to taste.

One of my previous development chef jobs involved working with airlines to create recipes that delivered on flavour when flying without solely adding lots of salt. Umami-rich ingredients, herbs and spices were my secret ingredients.

Tomato juice is the perfect example of a drink that has the taste-power of a jet engine – hence, why it's still so often drunk in the air.

Makes about 725ml/25fl oz spiced tomato juice; Serves 4

For the spiced tomato juice
700ml/1½ pints tomato juice
1 tbsp lemon juice
1 tsp diced jarred jalapeños
1 tsp light soft brown sugar
½ tsp grated (peeled) fresh
   horseradish root (optional)
Pinch of cracked black pepper
Dash of Tabasco sauce, or to taste
Dash of Worcestershire sauce,
   or to taste

For the Bloody Mary cocktails
Makes 4

For the celery salt
2 tbsp sea salt
1 tsp ground celery seeds
1 tsp dried chilli flakes

For the cocktails
Lemon wedges, for the glasses
Ice, to serve
1 x quantity (725ml/25fl oz) Spiced
   Tomato Juice (see above)
4 double shots (200ml/7fl oz) vodka
4 celery sticks
4 twists of lemon peel

For the spiced tomato juice, blend the tomato juice with all the other ingredients in a large blender, adding the Tabasco sauce drop by drop until you reach the desired spicy heat level and the dash of Worcestershire sauce last for umami levelling. Pour into a jug and chill in the fridge until ready to serve.

For the celery salt, using a pestle and mortar, grind the salt, ground celery seeds and chilli flakes together, then pour into a bowl to rim the cocktail glasses.

Chill the glasses in the freezer for 10–15 minutes, then rub the rims with lemon wedges. Dip/roll the rims in the celery salt (the chilling and lemon makes it easier for the salt to stick to the rims).

Add some ice to each glass. Pour the spiced tomato juice and vodka over the ice and garnish each cocktail with a celery stick to stir and a twist of lemon peel. Best served cold and spicy as a refined hair of the dog....

> ### Salt Geek
>
> *Celery salt (see above) is a useful store cupboard ingredient to have alongside your other flavoured salts. Make a large batch and store in a sealed jar in a cool, dark place for up to 12 months. Try using celery salt as an addition to mayo-laced potato salads, hard-boiled eggs, lobster dogs, hash browns or as a rub on chicken.*

Sea G&T with Seaweed Salt

My home, my Cornwall, has inspired this recipe. It's a cocktail that I think sums up the flavour of my local sea.

Makes 1 cocktail

For the sea spritz
(Makes about 100ml/3½fl oz)
3g/1/16oz sea salt flakes
1 tbsp aromatics – coriander seeds,
   dried juniper berries, fennel seeds,
   rose/pink peppercorns (optional)

For the seaweed salt
(Makes 1 small potful)
1 tbsp dried seaweed flakes
1 tbsp fine sea salt flakes

For the cocktail (Makes 1)
2 slices cucumber
Pinch of Seaweed Salt (see above)
Ice, to serve
Double shot (50ml/2fl oz) artisan gin
   (or non-alcoholic distilled botanicals)
150ml/¼ pint tonic water
Sprig fresh seaweed, to garnish

Prepare a spritz for this cocktail by dissolving the salt in 100ml/3½fl oz of water in a small pan over a medium heat. Add in any aromatics at this point if you are feeling adventurous. Leave to cool and infuse for 1–2 hours. Strain through a sieve and decant into a clean spray bottle. Store in the fridge for up to a week. Try using the spritz to season salads, spray on lamb as it grills or add it to a tofu marinade.

Mix the seaweed salt ingredients together in a small bowl.

For the cocktail, place the cucumber slices on a sheet of kitchen paper. Sprinkle a pinch of seaweed salt over the cucumber (keep the remaining seaweed salt in a sealed pot to use another time). Leave for 15–20 minutes. The salt will draw out some of the moisture and intensify the flavour of the cucumber without the slices diluting the cocktail.

Put some ice into a cocktail glass. Pour the gin (or botanicals) and tonic water over the ice and stir. Garnish with a sprig of seaweed and the salted cucumber slices. The seaweed-seasoned cucumber will reduce the bitterness of the tonic water and provide a briny, umami tang to the cocktail.

Spritz the rim of the glass with a fine spray of the infused brine before serving.

Smoked Toddy with Toast Salt

Perhaps my choice to include this drink here stems from memories of having a good craic with the Irish contingency of my family, gathered around the wood-burner and hearing funny stories of my dad when he was young. The other reason could simply be because the Hot Toddy is an unequivocally feel-good drink. To me, the combination of whiskey, orange and clove with sweet honey is near perfection. One of the few things I love more is toast.

This smoky comfort blanket of a drink blends two of my favourite flavours together and I hope you'll appreciate the complexity and cosiness. This recipe's ingredients also work extremely well with Lapsang Souchong instead of hot water as a cold brew smokehouse iced tea – it's worthwhile doing a summer version as tea on the rocks!

Makes 1 hot toddy

For the toast salt

1 slice bread

1 tbsp fine Smoked Sea Salt
  (see page 216)

1 tsp golden caster sugar

For the hot toddy

1 slice orange

50ml/2fl oz whiskey

1 tsp honey

1 slice orange, studded with 3–4 cloves

Sprig rosemary

1 cinnamon stick

Start by making the toast salt. Toast the slice of bread on both sides until it's dark brown and starting to burn, then use a knife to scrape off all the charred toast crumbs from the surface and crusts. You can eat the toast with some salted butter or turn it into breadcrumbs for another recipe. What you want to use for this recipe is the blackened toast crumbs scraped from the surface. Blitz the crumbs in a spice grinder with the smoked salt and sugar.

Prepare a heatproof glass for the hot toddy by rubbing the rim with the slice of orange and then dipping it in the toast salt.

For the hot toddy, heat 240ml/8½fl oz of water in a small pan to near boiling point (or use slightly cooled boiled water from the kettle). Pour the hot water into the prepared glass and add the whiskey, honey and the clove-studded slice of orange. Add the sprig of rosemary and cinnamon stick to serve. Stir together to dissolve the honey and leave to infuse for a minute. Carefully torch the sprig of rosemary (using a blowtorch) just before serving for a wonderful aromatic presentation that complements the smoked, salty toast rim.

Watermelon Margarita with Bamboo Salt

For my salty watermelon margarita, I wanted to capture the essence of a Tokyo night sky and neon psych vibe. The combination of charred fruit, sweet syrup or honey with a bright spirit is intoxicating. Bamboo salt provides a vegetal, grassy note to the cocktail. For me, bamboo salt has the dry, dusty, green flavour of walking under a midday canopy of leaves that shimmer and shadow the sky with bursts of sunshine blowing off the ocean. Give your margaritas a remix and get your blowtorch out alongside an intense-tasting artisan salt.

Makes 4 cocktails

For the cocktails

½ watermelon, peeled, de-seeded
    and cut into cubes

2 tsp caster sugar (optional)

125ml/4fl oz tequila

75ml/2½fl oz triple sec

Juice of 2 limes

2 tsp agave syrup

For the garnish

1 tbsp green bamboo salt (available
    to buy online) or make an equal mix
    of grated lime zest and sea salt

1 tsp caster sugar

1 lime, cut in half

4 small slices watermelon, for
    decorating the glass rims

For the cocktails, place the diced watermelon cubes on a baking tray and blowtorch, or place under a preheated hot grill for 2–3 minutes, until lightly charred. To speed up the char, you can lightly sprinkle them with the sugar. When the edges start to burn and caramelise, cool, then transfer the watermelon on a tray to the freezer and open-freeze overnight.

The next day, for the garnish, combine the bamboo salt (or lime zest and salt mix) and the sugar in a small saucer. Use the lime halves to rim the edge of four cocktail glasses and then dip each one in the combined salt/sugar mix. Set the rimmed glasses to one side. Char the watermelon slices (as before – see above) and allow to cool.

In a food processor, blitz the frozen charred watermelon cubes with the tequila, triple sec, lime juice and agave syrup. Pour the watermelon margaritas into the prepared glasses, garnish each glass with a charred watermelon slice, and enjoy.

Acknowledgements

For H.S. xxxxxxxx

I would like to dedicate this book to my wife Holly. Thank you for your love, support, advice and encouragement.

I'd also really like to thank some important people who've made this book possible.

Indiana, Pippin and Arrietty for introducing me to a pipkin of salt – the perfect amount for pumpkin soup. My mum Brigit Strawbridge for sharing her delicious sourdough recipe and for introducing me to Chelsea Green Publishing at her book launch party for *Dancing with Bees*. Also, thanks to her husband Rob for growing such delicious vegetables, which I used for many of the photographs. Thanks to my dad Dick Strawbridge and his wife Angela, too, for letting me come to the Chateau and cook up a feast on TV to showcase some flavoured salts.

Thanks also to Philip Tanswell from Cornish Sea Salt for sharing so much valuable Salt Geek knowledge with me over the years. My good friends Harry and Sarah for sharing your home kitchen with me for an intense day shoot and then taking some great photos of the cooking action, too – Harry you should shoot more photography! Julian, my literary agent at the Soho Agency, for setting up this publishing deal and helping to shape the idea of the book so it would appeal to a wider readership.

Next, I want to send over an extra huge thank you to both Matt Haslum and Muna Reyal from Chelsea Green Publishing for believing in this project and trusting in me to rewrite the narrative on salt. Your support and confidence have given me such a boost and I've hugely enjoyed working with you both – hopefully we can do this again one day? But next time not when I've got building work going on at home.... Anne Sheasby for working through all the queries that helped to tease out the detail at the copy editing stage, so the book hopefully now all makes sense. Big thanks to photographer John Hersey for shooting some stunning photography of me at my local hidden cove and for those special *Seasoned* shoots a few years ago when this book idea started to emerge – look forward to collaborating again soon. Ross Hoddinott for a fantastic landscape photography workshop. Woodrow Studios for some of the surface boards. Le Creuset for providing superb cookware.

I'd also like to mention Che and Callum who've been busy building a house for my mother-in-law Jan, while I was writing and shooting the book in my garden studio. I have really appreciated your positive energy and hard work which made the process a lot more noisy but less lonely.

I also just want to say thank you to all the clients at Strawbridge Kitchen who send me such good-quality ingredients to cook with, particularly Victoria Townsend from Ocean Fish. Recipe development is easy when you have good ingredients and I'm extremely lucky living in Cornwall to have some of the best food and drink to cook with.

Finally, thank you for taking the time to read this book – I hope you enjoyed it!
Cheers, James x

Index

Page numbers in *italic* refer to illustrations

Recipe Index

About the Author

James Strawbridge is a Cornish chef, photographer and sustainable living expert as well as the author of several cookbooks including *The Complete Vegetable Cookbook*, *The Artisan Kitchen* and *Practical Self-sufficiency* with Dick Strawbridge. Recent television presenting and appearances include *Escape to the Chateau* (Channel 4), *Strawbridge over the Drawbridge* (BBC) and *The Hungry Sailors* (ITV).